ECONOMICS

OF

WELFARE

DR. NAVODITA PANDE

Dedication

This book is dedicated to all my *family*, *friends* and *colleagues* who supported me and guided me to pursue my interest and

- ➤ For my illiterate **grandmother**, Jai Devi, who taught me to fight all odds

- ➤ For **Dr. Prannoy** and **Ms. Radhika Roy,** who taught me to always remain resilient and persevering

- ➤ For my **friend, Tara Roy,** for always believing in me and my abilities

- ➤ For my **daughter, Pranika,** who taught me every dawn brings a new day

- ➤ For the **Republic of India,** that taught me the beauty of evolution and growth

(that continues to inspire *me*)

Acknowledgements

This book is a reproduction of my doctorate. Throughout the doctoral journey, I have many people to thank for supporting me. Firstly, I want to thank God for the enablement to complete the doctoral degree. Through this inspirational time, the constant protection from God was outstanding as I was bringing up my daughter who was only two days' old.

Secondly, I would like to thank my supervisor and dissertation chair of my research, Professor Minja Bolesnikov, for the continuous support, advice, comments and critics, and encouragement throughout this dissertation's development. Thank you, prof. It would have been impossible to complete the research work without your guidance.

I am also grateful to SSBM management and staff for granting me the opportunity to study at a high-caliber business school, all the doctoral students and colleagues for their contribution during the study. The virtual lectures by Professor Anna Provodnikova proved to be insightful and helpful in managing and organizing my study.

Moreover, I would like to thank Adil Arshad from UpGrad, India, for offering valuable insights into my work and guide me through the financial procedure required to complete my studies. The virtual lectures organized by UpGrad, with mentors like Himanshu Manroa, Anil Ota and Brinda Sampat made me align my thoughts and ideas into a single coherent train of thought while researching. I also thank Eduvanz and Aditya Birla Group for helping me get a financial loan for completion of my studies. In this regard, I also thank my father, Mr. Krishna Chandra Pande, former tax official, for agreeing to pay my EMI (Equated Monthly Instalment) while I was rendered unemployed briefly in the process of writing my thesis. I also thank the Divine powers for guiding me through the writing stage as I stayed motivated and continued to write and make my submission as per the deadline.

Finally, I dedicate this doctoral degree to my family- mom Rekha, dad Krishna Chandra, daughter Pranika, brother Dhruv and sister-in-law, Nibedita for keeping me motivated and ensuring I am not disturbed while completing my dissertation. Their commitment and moral support contributed to completing the doctoral research. Thank you, and may God richly bless you all.

Introduction

India is a mixed economy since independence from the British. She, under the leadership of prime minister Jawaharlal Nehru, underwent a phase of expansion, expanding on the agricultural sector, manufacturing sector and the services sector. As years proceeded, Indian economy continued to remain mixed, being governed by the market forces under the capitalist structures and functioning in accordance with the socialist forces through government welfare schemes and public expenditure by various governments across different sectors. The study assesses these policies to devise a framework for existing good policies that facilitate economic development of India. The methods used for this study are semi-structured interviews of fifteen tax officials and lawyers who have sufficient knowledge of how taxation impacts the development of a country. There was an alternate hypothesis which was proven correct by the findings and results. In order to keep the study relevant, content analysis of the budget speech by finance minister Nirmala Sitharaman was conducted with different coding themes. These themes are studied, and the results are discussed below. Fifteen respondents had diverse opinions on how direct and indirect tax impacts development. Ten respondents believed that India is on the right growth trajectory with government policies that encourage discrete expenditure of public revenue for developmental purposes. Twelve respondents said that infrastructure should be the focus while allocating funds and resources for developmental tasks besides social alleviation of the marginalized in India. Content analysis results indicated the frequency of the words 'taxation' and 'development' in the budget speech by finance minister of India in July 2024. The words 'taxation' and 'development' were analysed as themes in the report with resultant discussions on taxation, public expenditure and economic development. Correlations were formed and results were linked to the literature review analysed under different themes. Thematic discussion led to different ideas about how tax-spend by governments impacts expenditure in the public domain and benefits citizens.

Keywords: Taxation; Direct tax; Indirect tax; Public expenditure; Government spending; Tax policy; Government policy; Economic policy; Economic development; Economic growth; Welfare state; Mixed economy; Fiscal policy; Indian economy; Taxation and development; Correlation; Content analysis; Interviews; neoclassical theory; Models of public expenditure.

Table of Contents

List of Tables

List of Figures

Chapter I

Introduction

1.1 Introduction

This study primarily aims to examine the impact of taxes on India's economic growth from 2019 to 2024. The country's economic activities in the fiscal year 2021–22 prompted the investigation because they raised the GDP. In 2022, the gross domestic product (GDP) reached 8.7 percent, thanks to the stimulus measures implemented by the government under the leadership of Dr. Nirmala Sitharaman (Cyrill, 2022). As a government measure to enhance economic development, it is critical to comprehend the monetary effects of taxes. Research in this area of developing economies will benefit from this study. Finding knowledge gaps about the effects of taxation systems, policies, and administration on India's economic growth definitions (both favorably and adversely) is the main impetus for this study. Knowledge advancement is aided by its findings, which will aid in the development of strategies for the country's future financial growth and provide policymakers and those involved in the process of defining and drafting fiscal policies with proposals and ideas. To that aim, we will be looking at the five-year plan from 2019 to 2024 to see if we can learn anything useful about how to manage our finances in the future.

According to the research, the country's previous financial officials had strong views and convictions. Important figures' remarks are considered, including those of the country's finance ministers, prime ministers' economic advisors, the head of the National Institution for Transforming India (NITI) Aayog, and the governor of the Reserve Bank of India.

1.2 Research Problem

Preliminary research shows that previous studies in India have mostly concentrated on trying to establish a connection between the country's tax system and its GDP development. Research shows that state economies feel the pinch of income and commodity-service taxes, but feel the full force of property and capital transaction taxes. Lowering income taxes should be the primary goal of policymakers. Additionally, it was discovered that some areas and states are considering modifying their tax systems to entice businesses or encourage growth. The World Tax Index also indicated that, in terms of the effect of taxes on GDP growth, personal income taxes, corporation taxes, social security contributions, and value-added taxes are in that order of severity. A systematic and all-encompassing analysis of the investment opportunities presented by income tax law to boost capital formation in the nation has been lacking from previous research.

Purpose of Research

The research's ultimate objective is to provide a theoretical model of the connection between the government's tax policy and India's economic growth. "Forcible transfer or payment of money from private individuals, institutions or groups to the government" is how Anyanwu (1999) describes a tax. "Transferring resources and income from the private sector to the public sector in order to achieve some of the nation's social and economic goals" is what taxation is, according to Okpe et al. (2011). "Compulsory payment made by individuals and corporate bodies to the government for financing government expenditure or for general purpose of government aimed at improving the taxpayers' welfare and in which both the taxpayer and the public at large benefit" is how Okwo et al. (2011) refer to taxes.

This research aims to fill a gap in the literature by surveying current practices in the taxation of various countries, particularly developing nations in Europe, Africa, and Asia.

1.3 Specific Aims

- o To provide a comprehensive review of sources and characteristics of tax framework in different countries.

- o To develop a theoretical model for the taxation framework of a country to steer it towards growth and development.

- o To review current industry practices and research in regard to taxation in countries with some of the best tax policies.

- o To outline a conceptual framework for total tax structures and financial growth.

1.4 Significance of the Study

Any government's economic policy that aims to promote economic growth and development must include taxation. Researching the interplay between taxation rules and economic structures across nations, as well as their most prominent tax structures and policies, is, consequently, crucial.

Taxation laws, tax structures, and tax policies as they relate to national economies are major developments in this area. A number of prominent thinkers have divergent views on the subject of India. According to Gandhi (1990), there are supply-side economists who are certain that lowering the tax burden and income tax rate significantly will affect growth rates and output levels. India, according to Pande (1996), has to change its tax rules and structure because it is a developing nation with low savings potential and is known to be a semi-industrialized nation. Furthermore, he states that nations that prioritize the private sector and have structured their taxes accordingly see faster economic growth compared to those that see the public sector as crucial to their development (ibid).

Some contend that income tax serves as a tool for advancing political, social, and economic policies in addition to generating cash. Since agricultural revenue is not subject to taxes, it does not seem fair to force 30% of the population to pay for 70% of the population's expenses (ibid). The relevance of the issue of the mutual interaction between taxes (tax burden) and economic growth (as a basic aim of economic policy makers) is highlighted by different approaches to the creation and characteristics of the tax system in relation to the budget problems of developed economies (Macek & Janku, 2015). Applying neoclassical growth theory to several tax systems, the author has sought to understand how each one promotes economic development. A number of prominent thinkers, like Judd (1987), have argued that a state's economic success is proportional to the efficiency of its government spending. According to the research article by King and Rebelo (1988), there are multiple causes of national differences and various tax policies implemented by governments serve to regulate these discrepancies. People are incentivized by their governments to amass physical and human capital. They found, among other things, that national tax policies affect private incentives to accumulate physical and human capital, which in turn affects the average rate of economic growth. They also found that the effects of national taxation depend on factors related to technology production for new human capital, and that tax policies can increase economic growth in the long run, which has a bigger quantitative impact on the state's welfare.

According to the Theory of Public Finance, unrestricted commerce with minimal constraints and a fundamental belief in laissez-faire are the workings of the free market. Problems of economic growth, planning, distribution, geographical inequities, and distributive justice have attracted the attention of economists since the inception of welfare economics (Bhatia & Ram, 2023). There are two common ways of looking at the tax problem: incentives and resources. The growth of the nation's economy depends on a reliable revenue system. Problems with an efficient tax system originate from the following, according to research (Ahmed & Gillwald, 2020):

- The economic structure

- The political economy of taxes

- The limited capacity for tax administration

- The poor quality of basic data

Financial stability and national progress can be better predicted with the help of this study's findings, which will be useful for practitioners in the field and relevant policymakers. So that taxes can have a positive effect on the economy, studies will identify which parts of the economy require a boost and which parts should receive the proper attention.

1.5 Research Purpose and Question/Hypothesis

The main research questions include:

RQ1: What is the impact of direct taxation on economic development?

RQ2: What is the impact of indirect taxation on economic development?

RQ3: What is the role of Goods and Services Tax (GST) on tax revenue collection of government?

RQ4: What is the role of startups and investments and their taxation in the business development of the country?

RQ5: How do such forms of taxation impact economic growth of the country?

The research questions help identify the research gaps and find answers and solutions to some important issues related to policy and development.

Chapter II

Literature Review

2.1 Introduction: Background of Taxation in India

Finding some big ideas and arguments on taxes and development from all around the world is the main goal of this literature study. As part of the literature review, we also looked at the many theoretical models and theories that have come before. This will help us with our current study, which will be carried out once the annual financial statement or budget for the fiscal year 2023-24 has been announced.

Tiwari (2018) assumes that tax rules influence India's economic activity and looks at the main debates over how taxes influence employment. Despite the fact that other variables impacting company site or job growth decisions impact employment in general, he argues that development projects financed by tax money will increase employment overall. Taxes that discourage investment and savings, on the other hand, make the economic downturn and unemployment problem worse. Thus, the Goods and Services Tax, an indirect form of taxation in India, may affect the country's GDP and jobless rate.

The Goods and Services Tax (GST) is an indirect tax system in India that Vasanthagopal (2011) claims has far-reaching economic consequences. At a specific GST threshold, it may safeguard the interests of merchants and enterprises within the MSME (Micro, Small and Medium Enterprises) sector, lower manufacturing costs for production units, increase agricultural prices benefiting farmers, and enable competition with Western equivalents. Furthermore, it is expected to alleviate poverty by lowering housing expenses through the reduction of imbedded taxes. As a means of reducing poverty, the Goods and Services Tax (GST) is supposedly not applied on food, healthcare, and educational services. Economic gains are also anticipated from improvements to land, labor, and capital, the three components of the production elements, as a result of GST. Here is a diagrammatic representation:

GST Taxation in India and its effects	Agriculture and manufacturing industry
	MSME and housing
	Poverty reduction and factors of production

Figure 1: Impacts of GST on the economy

Source: Vasanthagopal, 2011; 145

Hence it affects employment, EXIM (Export-Import) policy and trade, GDP and government revenue among other things.

2.2 Impact of Taxation on Tax Revenue and GDP

The three levels of government in India—the federal government, the states, and the rural or local bodies—are responsible for collecting taxes. Direct taxes, especially income tax, are largely responsible for the substantial growth in tax collections. According to Shrivastava et al. (2010), the tax-to-GDP ratio for the central government increased from 9.2% in 2003–04 to 11.5% in 2008–09. The authors of the 2008–09 Indian Economic Survey report argue that the central government's tax–to–GDP ratio increased by 46% from a low of 6.5% in 2002–03, with contributions from both direct and indirect taxes (ibid), despite the fact that the Indian economy was in recession during that fiscal year.

The tax collections in various years have been shown in a tabular form thus which indicate the contribution of the revenue collected to the overall development of the country:

Table 1: Tax Revenue (in % of GDP)

Year	% of GDP
2002-03	6.5
2003-04	6.8
2004-05	7.1
2005-06	7.5
2006-07	8.5
2007-08	9.3
2008-09 (BE)	9.5
2008-09 (RE)	8.8

Source: Economic Survey 2008-09, RE- Revised Estimates, BE- Budget Estimates

The percentage rise in tax revenue relative to GDP for 2006–07, 2007–08, and 2008–09 is shown clearly in the table. A possible diagram depicting the tax revenue structure as it pertains to various direct and indirect taxes could look like this:

2.2.1 Taxation as incentive and resources

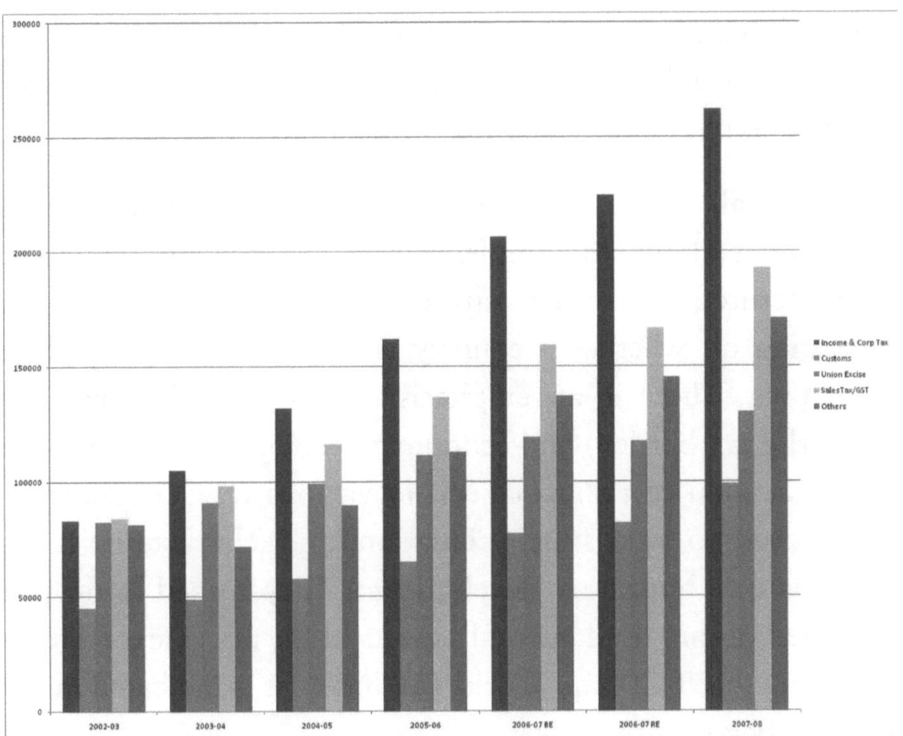

Figure 2: Tax revenue structures

Source: Economic Survey 2008-09

2.2.2 Taxation in Developed and Developing Countries

The incentives viewpoint and the resources viewpoint are two ways of looking at taxes and the problems it causes in terms of development (Kaldor, 1965). Some people think that low growth and investment are mostly due to a lack of incentives, hence they think that the tax system needs to be improved by giving more concessions of different kinds. Some people think that not having enough money means that development and investment aren't up to par. Their main objective is to raise taxes in order to boost investment capital (ibid).

Many developing countries' economies suffer, according to Kaldor (1965), because of a lack of tax income and a lack of rational planning for allocating public funds.

Countries all across the world have their own unique ways of thinking about and implementing tax systems. Different tax structures and systems are determined in different ways depending on whether a country is considered developed or developing. There is an emphasis on the interplay between taxes (the tax burden) and economic development and growth (the basic goal of policymakers) in various OECD countries' approaches to tax system creation and characteristics as they relate to budgetary development. They zeroed in on and identified certain fundamental aspects of the tax categorization according to OECD and World Tax Index. It is indicated in the diagram below:

Table 2: Tax classification according to OECD and WTI

OECD	WTI
Personal income taxes	Personal income taxes
Corporate income taxes	Corporate income taxes
Social security contributions	Value added tax

OECD	WTI
Property taxes	Property taxes
Value added tax	Other taxes on consumption
Other taxes on consumption	

Source: **Macek (2014), Kotlan & Machova (2012), Macek & Janku (2015)**

According to this research, there needs to be a proper way to evaluate tax burdens because different tax systems have different features, such as national specifications. In this study, we compare and contrast two taxation models, the neo-classical growth model and certain tax burden approximation methods. We find that, up to a steady state, capital accumulation increases the rate of product growth. However, it was also shown that government spending has a detrimental effect on economic growth. The following are further noteworthy findings:

- OECD countries should lower their tax rates.

- To make up for the drop in income tax receipts, it is necessary to raise indirect taxes.

On the flip side, studies conducted on emerging nations, mostly in Latin America, have shown that economies in the region benefit from a greater reliance on consumption taxes, according to Canavire-Bacarreza et al. (2013). According to Neog (2018), developing nations like India greatly benefit from fiscal policy. Governments use tax systems to collect money and deal with problems like inflation, price stability, and employment. They also use them to measure things like GDP, the balance of payments, and how wealth is distributed fairly. By applying the framework of optimum tax policy theory to a number of articles, the author concludes that, when applied to India, tax policy always affects growth performance (ibid).

Measures like tax buoyancy and elasticity of taxation, which in turn affect income elasticity, suggest that taxes, particularly indirect taxes like sales tax, affect national growth.

Taxes are not the only source of revenue for the government. Additional sources of public or government revenue include mineral royalties, net revenues from marketing boards, and public-sector profits, as described in Section 3.2. At present, these revenue streams from the government can be classified as taxes, and they should be assessed in the same way. Governments can meet their financial commitments through a variety of channels, such as taxation, borrowing money either domestically or abroad, or even creating new currency. There are benefits and drawbacks to using other sources of funding. Finding a balance between taxation, borrowing, and money creation is what the next section is all about.

There are a number of reasons why the government does or does not do anything when it comes to managing public expenditure.

(i) Conditions that inhibit completely competitive behavior include imperfect knowledge, rising returns, entry obstacles, and missing markets; this also includes externalities and public goods.

(ii) The distribution of income and poverty: results, efficient or not, may cause some people to suffer incredible poverty or produce an undesirable distribution.

(iii) Right to education, health, nutrition, and housing: the lack of these factors greatly limits an individual's capacity to participate in the economy and society; thus, it can be argued that "equality of opportunity" requires the state to ensure basic nutrition, literacy, housing, and health care.

(iv) Paternalism: The state may believe it knows better than individuals what's best for themselves, leading it to believe it should take precedence over human choices in some situations. School attendance requirements, drug use limits, etc., are relevant instances.

The well-being and rights of subsequent generations may be inadequately considered when individuals put their own interests and those of their descendants first. The preservation of rainforests, the protection of species, and the mitigation of air and water pollution are all pertinent instances. There is a strong case for government action in each of the above points. Infrastructure, social security, education, health, pensions, and the environment are just a few of the areas where the government spends money, and the examples given also show how the government helps keep the economy competitive. When it comes to infrastructure, like power and communications, where increasing returns, public goods, and externalities are major factors, arguments against market failure are especially strong. In addition, for the economy to function competitively, there must be legal and regulatory frameworks in place to guarantee well-defined and respected property rights, to enforce contracts, and to restrict unlawful activity. Basic administration, maintaining law and order, and defense are also essential components of these responsibilities. Although this analysis of the pro-state arguments draws attention to important and expensive areas where the state could step in, the arguments put forth do not provide sufficient evidence to support the idea that the state should directly intervene in the production of consumer and producer goods (for more information, see Stern 1992).

Again using Tait (1999), it is worth noting that domestic taxes on goods and services have been declining in significance in industrialized nations, while VAT has been growing in importance. There is mounting evidence that VAT will maintain its upward trajectory due to its many perceived benefits, such as a large base covering a wide range of goods and services, neutrality regarding both domestic and international trade, and challenges associated with evasion.

To avoid the system from becoming too complicated, excise taxes should only be applied to a small subset of items. Instead, most products should be subjected to a unified indirect taxation system, like VAT. The central excise system in India is a form of general production taxation with very varied rates. It seems like a good idea to develop a value-added tax system that covers most items (Ahmad et al., 1991; Cnossen, 1992). Foreign trade taxes bring in 29.4 percent of all tax revenue in developing nations, which is 5.1% of GDP. As a result, their importance is on par with that of domestic taxes on goods and services (30.4%) and income taxes (5.5% and 28.9%, respectively). They only account for 0.7% of GDP and 2.8% of total tax income in industrialized nations, so their impact is small. The principal justification for implementing trade tariffs is their administrative feasibility, as will be shown in Section 4. Most people think they aren't very efficient. Developing nations with incomes between $360 and $750 have the greatest trade taxes relative to GDP, while those with incomes between $1620 and $6000 have the lowest.

With only 1.3% of GDP and 6.2% of tax income going toward social security, developing nations' contributions are negligible. This is in stark contrast to industrialized nations, where they contribute a substantial portion of tax income (28.4% of total revenue) and 8.9% of GDP. It is important to recognize the substantial difficulties in establishing formal social security systems in developing countries, but this should not be taken as an indication that social security is not a high priority there. Burgess and Stern (1991) found that collecting social security payments was just as difficult as collecting income taxes from individuals. Consequently, coverage is sometimes not available to workers in rural regions or the informal sector, unlike in industrialized nations where it is almost universal (for discussion, see Ahmad et al., 1991; and Atkinson et al., 1989). In emerging nations, wages make up the bulk of the social security tax base. The share of GDP attributable to wages grows in tandem with the level of per capita income. As a result, there is a highly significant positive relationship ($r=0.48$, $p<1\%$) between the proportion of GDP that goes toward these taxes and log GNP per capita.

Administrative shortcomings and tax evasion continue to be major problems in many countries, even if they receive substantial tax revenues. For administration to run well, many nations believe that a solid legislative foundation must first be put in place. Government policy must be consistent, open, and honest if improvements are to maintain popular support. The consolidation of several kinds of taxes into one administrative structure has made data gathering and enforcement more easier. Some nations, like Indonesia, have successfully used self-assessment for income tax reasons, while value-added tax systems give authorities a strong audit trail. The costs will still be there even when the public sector is no longer responsible for them. Many smaller companies see value-added tax as a huge obstacle.

The taxation structure in developing countries drastically differs from that in affluent countries. Nearly two-thirds of tax revenue in emerging nations comes from indirect taxes, with domestic and trade taxes contributing almost equally. The corporate income tax makes up the majority of the latter one-third. Direct taxes, which mostly include income taxes and social security contributions, account for about two-thirds of a developed country's revenue. Although developing nations follow an average structure, there is a great deal of diversity in the sources of income among them. Domestic sales taxes appear to be gradually replacing trade taxes as a result of domestic economies developing and enabling the creation of tax instruments targeted at domestic output and transactions. As a share of GDP and tax revenue, personal income taxes have changed over time, although in some nations they have stayed about the same or even gone down.

In response to policy successes and the rise of analytical economics, studies examining the relationship between taxes and development have made great strides in the previous 20 to 30 years. Many structural adjustment challenges revolve around tax reform and spending control. In the absence of budgetary stability, structural adjustment is doomed to fail. Recognizing the necessity of new tax systems, nations in Eastern Europe, the former Soviet Union, and elsewhere that are loosening or eliminating tight economic regulations must proceed with caution. Both developed and developing nations can benefit much from learning from the theoretical lessons and real-world experiences of the other.

2.2.3 The Impact of Taxes on the Economy and Employment

Labor taxation and labor market outcomes have been the subject of a great deal of theoretical and empirical research, with a wide range of institutional features of different labor markets taken into account. These features include, but are not limited to, regulations pertaining to employment protection, unemployment benefits, minimum wages, skill levels, wage rigidity, and wage bargaining structures. Several of the most important macro-level empirical research will be briefly summarized in this section. Both de Haan, Sturm, and Volkerink (2003) and Nickell (2003) as well as Macek (2014) provide summaries of these investigations. According to Macek (2014), lowering taxes on labor might boost employment and demand for labor by encouraging businesses to hire more people and, in particular, by lowering wages for low-wage workers. To improve productivity and advance the EU's economic framework as a whole, an employment-friendly wage must be implemented (European Commission 2005). Reducing social security contributions for disadvantaged groups, adjusting personal income tax thresholds, modifying self-employment contribution regulations, increasing nominal wages, changing minimum wage and social security legislation, and a number of other measures have been put in place by many Member States to reduce the tax wedge. Carone et al. (2005) and the quarterly reports of the European Employment Observatory (http://www.eu-employmentobservatory.net) provide further information on measures across EU Member States. There are two sides to the supply and demand for labor, and both sides impose taxes on it. Income taxes are levied on workers, while companies are required to pay payroll taxes and social security contributions. As a rule, it is believed that the side on which a tax is levied has no bearing on the incidence of that tax on labor. The treatment of income and payroll tax rates is often considered to be equal in empirical investigations of wage formation. Furthermore, it is common for theoretical analyses of tax incidence and wage formation to fail to distinguish between income and payroll taxes. According to studies, domestic and foreign nominal salaries fall as a consequence of a compensatory rise in domestic tax progression, which keeps government tax income stable. This is good news for employment in both countries. The income tax rate has a negative substitution effect on the wage rate, which leads to this significant conclusion. Foreign wage rates fall as a consequence of falling domestic wage rates because falling domestic wage rates boost domestic product supply and cause foreign currency to appreciate. The outcome is a fall in the value of the currency, which in turn leads to a decrease in the pay set by the monopoly union abroad. Though they have different impacts on wages in reality, income and payroll taxes are often treated as one and the same in theoretical investigations of tax incidence and wage formation. When the income tax base is constrained owing to tax exemptions, the study by Holm and Koskela (1996) shows that domestic gross earnings and employment fall as a result of a neutral restructuring of labor taxes from the employer's home country. The function of labor taxes cannot be well described by this situation. Restructuring that does not affect revenue has no effect on foreign employment if the income tax base remains constant. Higher gross wages are the consequence of coordinated changes to tax parameters, more pure progression in both nations, and the codification of labor taxes. This, in turn, makes it possible for employment transitions within specific countries to increase, especially in cases where tax breaks are in place.

2.2.4 Employment Effects of Taxation in OECD Countries

The efficiency impacts of taxes have been mainly disregarded in comparative welfare state studies. Iversen and Wren (1998) and Kenworthy (2013) focused on the revenue side of things and looked at how redistribution affected growth and employment. A growing body of literature (e.g., Steinmo, 2002; Swank, 1998; Hallerberg & Wagschal, 1998) examines welfare state financing. When it comes to job performance, Scharpf (2000) breaks it down by country and by time. His analysis includes both the independent variable "taxes" and the dependent variable "employment." Because of this, he is able to zero in on the details of taxes and how they affect industries that are very amenable to changes in tax policy.

The study finds that private sector employment is negatively affected by some types of taxes, particularly social security contributions and indirect taxes, based on an analysis of cross-sectional data from thirteen OECD nations. Industries like manufacturing, which are exposed to global markets, are less affected by tax changes than services that require low to intermediate skill inputs.The traditional microeconomic view of the labor supply serves as the basis for analyzing the impact of taxes. labor may be supplanted by more leisure, other sources of income, or even more labor in the future as a consequence of taxes, all else being equal (Gustafsson 1996). Goods that need less effort to produce may also become more popular as a result. The main cause is the difference between the gross and net wages. The availability of workers is affected by a decrease in the net wage. Only when taxes on income are more than offset by substitution can the labor supply rise. According to micro econometric research, income effects (IE) are more significant than substitution effects (SE) for some demographics, including single moms (Blundell 1995). At the macro level, for complete economic sectors or the job market overall, a conventional situation is expected. There should be some elasticity in the labor supply. However, this could be a warning sign about the gender gap in economic sectors across countries, which could distort the results of studies. A textbook-style examination of labor supply is made more complicated by the presence of numerous real-world factors. Different countries have different fixed costs of labor. According to Esping-Andersen (2010), the cost of childcare is much greater in continental Europe as compared to North America and Scandinavia.

The features of a welfare state impact even the most fundamental economic models, as this shows. Even in a closed economy, the analytical framework becomes much more complicated when a macro view of the labor market is adopted. Wages are thought of as being malleable; for instance, the effect of a rise in payroll tax will depend on how elastic the supply of labor is. Net wages fall when supply is inelastic and employment falls when supply is perfectly elastic (Gustafsson 1996: 836). According to Hamermesh (2005), who examined a large body of empirical evidence, salaries are the principal object of taxation. Employers might shift the expense of labor onto workers when looking at the big picture. Reducing payroll or general taxes, according to Bauer and Riphahn (1998), would have a negligible impact on employment and unemployment rates in Germany's labor market.This problem is closely related to the existence of unemployment in a labor market. Qualitative mismatch is a symptom of structural unemployment, which makes it harder for the job market to react to changes in tax policy. As the only type of "reservation wages," unemployment benefits are closely linked to taxes in neoclassical models of the labor market.

According to Kemperling (2002), the wage bargaining mechanism is unaffected by changes in taxes. The problem with these models, though, is that redistribution is a component of many social security systems. There are other forms of social transfers besides taxation. An rise in overall taxes could lead to lower employment rates and higher unemployment rates in certain cases.5 The "efficiency-wage" model and other alternative economic theories of unemployment posit that payroll taxes have a negative impact on employment through causing the equilibrium wage rate to move further away from the market-clearing point (Phelps 1994; Pissaridis 1998).High tax rates, according to a dynamic viewpoint, slow economic growth and raise capital-to-labor ratios in the long run. The result is a decline in job opportunities (Kemmerling, 2002). Taxation affects unemployment in more ways than one, according to Daveri and Tabellini (2000). Different wage-bargaining institutions are considered crucially important by the writers. In continental Europe, where taxation makes real wage increases more of a priority, the negative impact of taxes on employment is greatest. Unemployment in these countries is mostly attributable, according to the authors, to the high cost of labor caused by labor taxes (Daveri & Tabellini 2000).

2.2.5 Macro institutional Approach of Tax Regimes

Insights from comparative studies on welfare states will be integrated with economic analysis of tax-mixes in this part. The first of the three stages is on the connection between the two halves of the public budget, which are revenues and expenditures. Here we assume that the welfare state system is really two separate regimes, one of which is taxes and the other is social transfers. Hence, social expenditures are important to the causal mechanisms that link taxes to the labor market, even though they aren't explicitly taken into account when analyzing the tax-employment relationship. The best first step, quantitatively speaking, would be to "net out" social payments and taxes so that we have accurate data on individual incentives, but this isn't without its difficulties. One distinguishing feature of welfare states that this viewpoint fails to take into account is the high degree of "tax churning" involved in providing public benefits (Armingeon & Beyeler, 2004). Many people's personal funds are redirected by welfare governments, and the reasons for this are frequently complicated and hard to pin down. According to Ademas (2008), there is a lot of empirical work that goes into constructing net government budgets. An alternate method is utilized in this investigation. There is an initial effort to link tax systems with the social transfer system, but now it's all about taxes. The next stage is to look at the tax systems of OECD countries historically. Notable variations among nations with similar tax loads will be shown by this. This leads us to wonder if there is a relationship between the three groups of welfare states and the ways in which tax systems vary. Last but not least, we must examine the consequences of different tax regimes on labor market results and reintegrate the tax system into labor markets. Some welfare state funding techniques may have a negative impact on employment and perhaps increase the unemployment rate. Particularly contrasting the industrial sector with the low-skilled service sector, the conversation draws attention to the difference between shielded and exposed economic sectors. Finally, it discusses how the "tax-employment link" has changed throughout time.A methodical approach to studying the interplay between various forms of social transfer and taxation. A stylized budget for a hypothetical representative welfare state is laid forth in the document. From a revenue perspective, there are three main types of taxes: income taxes (INCTAX), indirect taxes (INDTAX), and payroll taxes (PAYTAX). These do not include other sources of governmental income.

There are three distinguishing features of each type of tax system: the degree to which it is progressive in relation to income, the extent to which it covers all individuals in terms of the number of people it affects, and the existence of discrimination between people, especially between married couples and single earners. Several substantial types of passive social transfers are part of the spending side. Once again, different types of social transfers and, most importantly, other types of government spending are not included. In most countries, the five main types of social transfers make up more than 60% of all government spending, or more than two-thirds of the social budget. The three main characteristics linked to these transfers are identified by standard comparative welfare state analysis (e.g., Esping-Andersen 1990). The primary differentiation is between social transfers that "status-preserving" and those that "status-reversing" aim to do. One type of transfer that helps people out equally while they're working and when they're not is public pension systems and unemployment payments. Specific social transfer eligibility requirements are handled in the second property. One common way to define this difference is in terms of universal vs means-tested benefits. Each of the five types of social transfers has its own set of requirements for eligibility. If you're unemployed and looking for work, you can be eligible for unemployment benefits, although health benefits are more commonly linked with sickness. The third quality is related to how different social transfer systems handle families. Some public pension schemes, for instance, treat married people differently than unmarried people.Particularly when it comes to income taxes, national policy methods display a great deal of variability (Ganghof 2000).

While some nations' income tax systems are designed to be more family-friendly and use a joint-taxation system, others have different rules for married couples. To broaden their revenue base, some nations levy taxes on social transfers. When looking at these countries from a net perspective, the differences between neoliberal welfare states and what appear to be generous welfare states, such as the Netherlands and Denmark, are not big (Adema 2008). Some governments use more traditional approaches, such direct income subsidies, to execute social policies; others, like the United States and the United Kingdom, use negative income taxation in various forms. Both the social security system and the welfare regime rely on the taxation system. Countries have different property distributions and tax and social transfer percentages. This is why the balance sheet is so basic and streamlined.There are significant similarities between societal transfers and taxation. There is a major difference that divides these into two groups. All taxes (direct and indirect), welfare (social assistance), and child benefits fall into one group. Because of the redistribution of funding, these do not maintain status. Unemployment benefits and state pensions are examples of expenses that are funded through payroll taxes. Taxes and entitlements are equal since they are both tied to earned income. On this spectrum, we find public health insurance, which, in most cases, offers universal in-kind benefits to all citizens and usually shows a linear relationship with income. Secondly, family-focused social benefits and the idea of joint taxes have certain similarities.

Both programs uphold the welfare model that relies on men to provide for their families. When compared to systems that treat everyone fairly, welfare states that prioritize families stand out. In the end, it seems that means-testing and other conditioning methods work well with both generous and generously redistributive top-down policies. They usually aren't compatible with status-preserving transfers. As an example, public pensions are a hot topic, with governments across the OECD working to restrict early retirement and regularly changing transfer eligibility requirements. Unlike other forms of government assistance, unemployment benefits are conditional on the recipient actively seeking employment, making them a special instance. The well-documented internal contradictions between the two concepts spark heated disputes over how to activate individuals in their search behavior. This tax-transfer mechanism framework takes into account factors that are frequently disregarded while analyzing welfare states.

Within its purview are wage taxes (both indirect and direct) and "reservation wages." Also included are social policy projects that receive all of their funding from the government. This field places a premium on tax breaks and exemptions for social goals. On the other hand, social policy that is dictated from on high by the state is a separate issue (Adema 2008). Saint-Paul (1996) argues that non-monetary labor market restrictions are the guiding principles of these social policies, which make them difficult to incorporate into existing tax and social transfer systems.

2.2.6 Tax-employment Links in OECD Countries

There has been a noticeable shift in the "tax-employment" relationship. High taxes is seen as a disadvantage when compared to other economies, according to the standard reasoning about internationalization, taxation, and employment. Since goods markets are competitive on a global scale, higher taxes push up the cost of non-wage labor, which in turn forces businesses to close their doors. According to Scharpf (2000), this effect is unnecessary if productive companies can reduce their net wages and pass the savings on to their employees. Levels of labor productivity may be endogenous to taxes, which complicates the evaluation of this claim. If this is so, businesses in protected industries are less likely to lay off workers due to high taxes than their internationally exposed counterparts. As a result, the competitive sectors may have been more tax sensitive in the past, even though they seem to be tax insensitive now. Has economic globalization altered "the rules of the game" for contemporary welfare states? This is an intriguing subject to ponder. Central banks, businesses, and trade unions largely fought and resolved the 1970s crisis over wage policy, according to Scharpf (2000). Here, he says, things are different for welfare states than they were in the 1990s, when capital and goods markets were far more integrated and so more difficult to reverse. Consequently, differences in welfare state regimes should be more significant now than they were before the oil crisis. A potential guiding concept for further investigation could be the adoption of tax and welfare regimes, assuming the premise that institutions now matter is valid. The "employment-friendly" tax system of Scandinavian welfare states mitigates some of the negative effects of heavy taxation, claims Scharpf (2000). When compared to welfare states in continental Europe, those in Anglo-America have the lowest rates of overall taxation and the highest rates of "employment-harming" taxes, making them the least effective at creating jobs. Scharpf breaks down total employment into its component parts in order to assess the employment-friendliness of various tax categories. One can classify all private or corporate jobs as either "sheltered" or "internationally exposed" (2000a: 197). Services geared toward the general public, such as food service, social assistance, and retail and wholesale commerce, make up the bulk of the sheltered sector. Utilities, manufacturing, and production-oriented service industries, including finance, make up the exposed sector. These differences are useful because they allow us to categorize the prevalent skill sets and the intensity of international rivalry. Companies in non-tradable industries with a high concentration of low-skilled workers and low productivity would be hit the hardest by taxes if only companies with a higher average level of workforce qualification could raise taxes on consumers (ibid.: 210).8 Similarly, the negative effect on employment in these low-skill sectors is not uniform among the three major types of taxes. There ought to have been a greater effect of taxes on employment in general if the globalization hypothesis is correct. By erecting trade barriers, a closed economy may shield certain industries from competition and keep its tax rates far higher than those of other countries.

2.3 Theoretical Framework

A free market mechanism is postulated in the Theory of Public Finance, which is based on a preference for unrestricted trade and a firm belief in the principles of laissez-faire. Concerns about economic development, planning, distribution, geographical inequalities, and distributive justice have piqued the interest of economists since the advent of welfare economics (Bhatia, 2023). There are two common ways to look at the tax problem: incentives and resources. The growth of a country's economy is directly related to how well its tax system works. According to research by Ahmed and Gillwald (2020), there are several basic problems with tax systems that make them ineffective.

- How the economy is structured

- Limitations on tax administration capacity

- Low quality of basic data

- Taxation as it relates to political economy

The essential character and necessity of taxes are called into doubt by this. In this context, the term "tax" has a range of accepted definitions. According to Anyanwu (1999), taxation is the process via which private entities are obligated to hand over a portion of their wealth to the state. According to Okpe et al. (2017), taxation is the process by which a country's social and economic goals are met by redirecting funds and assets from private companies to the public sector. According to Okwo (2022), taxation is "the obligatory outlay of monetary resources by individuals or entities for the purpose of funding general governmental expenditures or improving the well-being of taxpayers," which in turn benefits society as a whole.

The first group of "private" goods, according to Samuelson et al. (1980), are priced according to ordinary market forces and do not have the "external effects" that collective consumption goods do. Therefore, benefit-theory based taxes cannot decentralize computational issues as effectively as the second group of goods. There is little doubt that ideal voting and signalling systems are conceivable. The problem with market catallactics does not disprove the claim that, given enough information, the best course of action can be determined by considering all potential world states and selecting the one that is considered most beneficial in light of the preexisting ethical welfare function. This is demonstrated by frameworks such as the "Scandinavian consensus," Kant's "categorical imperative," and others that are relevant only when "symmetry" is present. The key is to find it, yet the answer is already there. Community members could be trained to behave as "parametric decentralised bureaucrats," communicating their preferences via price parameter signals, Lagrangean multipliers, surveys, or some other means. At the heart of social economy, nevertheless, lies a crucial technical difference: people might seek personal gain in ways that are impossible under the self-regulating competitive pricing of private commodities if they stray from the rules. In addition, the grand system of optimizing equations cannot reach the precise pattern of zeros required for laissez-faire competition to be theoretically feasible as an analog computer due to the "external economies" or "jointness of demand" that are inherent to collective goods and governmental functions. It is common for detractors to overlook welfare economics' practical applications. It is true that it has failed to accomplish its goals: it has not shown that laissez-faire is better, it has not provided clear standards for judging economic changes or ideal circumstances, and it has not shown how to separate the economic and ethical aspects of policy. These goals are so lofty that they will be impossible to reach. Achieving less lofty analytical goals requires welfare economics.

Individuals or groups' economic welfare can be seen as a single metric that is likely related to the expected enjoyment of products while also taking into account the hazards that come with them. This sort of result is not reliably produced by economic analysis tools; for real-world applications, it is necessary to tailor the objective function to the analysis. In the long run, a public works program can help the economy, reduce local poverty, lessen the impact of natural disasters, pave the way for new parks and other recreational spaces, and even add some internationally and domestically significant monuments to the landscape.

A disorganised merger or the neglect of all aims other than expected concrete benefits could emerge from depending on single welfare metrics. Assuming a scalar utility function exists, it is possible to reduce different outputs to common units for each person. However, in reality, the many effects need to be organized into important goal categories. Economic conditions, for example, can be seen as differentiating factors between depression benefits, which are more tied to timing and the employment and purchasing power created, and full employment benefits, which can be measured through market data. Another factor is the tangibility of the effect, or whether it can be measured objectively or is subject to arbitrary valuation. The accuracy of the predictions, differentiating between outputs that satisfy explicit requirements and those that are dependent on a variety of reverberation effects; and the delivery of the benefits, classifying the often-uncertain distant benefits as a separate benefit category. Experts in policymaking rarely see the problems they face as unique. They see the world more clearly through the lens of a multiple objective function. In particular, it gives them charge of prioritizing the goals and delivering the technical analysis's findings in the most practical way. It is up to the policymaker and the technologist to settle the dispute about how specific the goals should be. On the other hand, the technician shouldn't try to take on the task of objective weighting by offering a one-size-fits-all answer and making the weighting procedure seem complicated with too many technical details.

The concept of benefits is necessarily relative because the objective function is sometimes multidimensional and must connect with the problem at hand. The definition of benefits is simple under specific assumptions. In a perfect market free from external economies or diseconomies in production and consumption, prices accurately reflect benefit under full employment, when the marginal utility of income is uniform across individuals. Assuming that the marginal utility of income is consistent across individuals and remains constant over the spectrum of variation, a simple conclusion can be drawn if a project is big enough to affect the prices of its outputs. A good indicator of benefits is the area under the production demand curve. By taking the average of the old and new prices and multiplying it by the number of units sold, we may quantify the benefit, assuming the curves are linear. Here is an additional interesting example: if we suppose that the individual indifference curves are hyperbolic, then Fischer's "ideal" index number indicates that there is a benefit. Benefit is not always easy to pin down. Assuming a cardinal notion linked with willingness to pay, it is theoretically possible to measure the change in individuals' utility. But in reality, this is a huge undertaking that calls for the creation of expedient methods. When trying to estimate benefits, the question of which chains of consequences to take into account naturally emerges. As a general rule, it is not possible to estimate the benefits when public services are genuine social goods.

Scenarios with well-defined goals and the main economic problem of minimizing the real cost of achieving them provide examples with wide applicability, particularly in the field of operations research. This poses a fascinating economic challenge with various unique ways to accomplish the goals. Several optimisation techniques, such as linear programming, simulation, or the neoclassical theory of the firm (which derives the theorem about marginal productivities), can be used to analyze the problem. Although these methods are not covered in detail in this work, the importance of public expenditure analysis is highlighted. Economics can still play a role in this context, even though benefit estimation is not possible due to the nature of common goods.

2.3.1 Constraints and the Theory of Budgeting

Limitations are not always a good indicator of how things really work in an organization. Except for short periods, budgets are not set in stone; even then, more appropriations can happen. The need for an operation to be self-liquidating is one example of a financial criterion that is seldom met when circumstances change. Loosening restrictions is likely to occur if they pose a substantial obstacle to achieving economic welfare. However, financial limitations are a powerful instrument for analysis. By limiting some or all available funds, it seeks to answer the following question: How best to put these constraints to use? After that, the analysis decides how to best distribute the limited funds. When used to a program, this method reliably reveals which resource limits its size. The difficulties can be assessed by a government agency that is responsible for allocating funds from higher authorities or by a planning commission in a developing country that is trying to come up with an investment strategy with limited resources (both domestic and international). In this context. Budgeting theory is based on the principle of limitations.

It is preferable to critically assess constraints rather than accept them without question. Even when there is a ceiling on spending in a given budget, it is still critical to distribute the limited resources as efficiently as possible. To make sure the marginal expenditures are beneficial, it's necessary to do another evaluation. The benefits should be equivalent to what would be received if the monies were spent outside of the budget.

2.3.2 Prices versus Interdependence Recognized

Careful consideration of advantages and costs must go into selecting the chain of effects to be sought when building an analytical framework to optimize a certain objective function. A key component of public spending economics is the precise characterization of the analysis. Numerous positive societal consequences, both measurable and otherwise, can be easily identified. On the other hand, it's easy to cave in to the perfect market process to the point that you stop caring about the bigger picture. As of right now, there is just one method in economics for determining what field of study is suitable. The model of perfect competition is used to start the analysis. Because prices in this model are proportional to the marginal rates of change in production and consumption, they are reliable measures of worth. After all, the market system guarantees a good distribution of resources, thus thinking about consequences outside the market is unnecessary. Some consequences should be thought about because there is no such thing as ideal competition in the actual world. To prove a case under this framework, one must show how the specifics differ from the ideal of competition. There is a wide variety of consequences. There is a small and gradually disappearing conservative bias in measuring these impacts when perfect competition is used as a starting point. Cases with substantial consequences are becoming more and more identified by economists working on developing nations. Giving concrete form to the "social" impacts from an individualist welfare economic standpoint, the inclusion of consequences must be justified in order to improve the analysis and lay the groundwork for empirical assessment.

2.3.3 Structural Unemployment and Underemployment

The expenditure choice model needs to take into account the fact that in developing countries there aren't enough jobs or jobs with low productivity. It may be necessary to employ a "adjusted" wage—which could be zero—in order to maximize national income as regular money-wages do not properly reflect opportunity costs. In addition, the goal function should heavily emphasize job creation, necessitating separate quantitative analysis to assess project performance, including jobs created in subsequent stages of production; input-output analysis serves this role admirably.

The unpredictable and dangerous nature of the economic environment must be considered in some way by expenditure criteria. The field of welfare economics lacks a comprehensive framework for handling risk and irrelevant optimal conditions that may be used as decision-making criteria. However, certain methods will be suggested, and it is easy to prove that risk must be included for many sensible objective functions. While weighing the pros and cons of these risk and uncertainty mitigation strategies, it is important to remember that more security comes at the cost of some other benefit, and that, looking at the big picture, the country may not benefit most from making short-term modifications. If, for instance, the hypothesis of a risk premium holds water empirically—that is, that hazardous investments must have a comparatively higher projected gain—then, despite the increased risk, the national income will increase more when risky investments are made. A greater national income and longer-term security could be achieved by a sequence of high-risk, high-reward investments rather than a series of low-risk investments. Accordingly, while there is a compelling argument for a number of changes aimed at secure behaviors, the cumulative effect of these changes might be counterproductive.

2.3.4 Maximization of Expected Utility

One can find the utility function that maximizes the expected value by following Bernoulli. If the function is not linear, meaning that marginal utility is constant, then the optimal analysis will use the probability distribution of outcomes. There is a common belief that the most logical course of action when faced with risk is to maximize predicted benefit. It is not an exhaustive explanation of human nature, but as a descriptive hypothesis it is amenable to empirical testing. However, it might accomplish the same goal as the traditional consumer theory when it comes to normative welfare economics—providing a prescription for what a rational consumer ought to do. Choosing which individual(s) to apply the approach's utility function to is an issue when dealing with public spending. Is it the planner's or the affected people's utility function? Choosing an interest rate is similar to this challenge. The roles of individuals ought to be utilized and given some consideration from an entirely individualist ethical standpoint. The collective may endure less harm than an individual when it comes to risk-related utility loss, such as when it comes to mortality-related projected utility loss. As a result of combining the results, the overall variance may be lower than that of the separate components.

Insisting on utility function specification requires us to be ready to put this theory into practice empirically. This is a difficult but inevitable problem, since even in classical models, it is likely that implicit estimations of utility functions would be required to specify disaster income levels or confidence probability levels. It is possible to generate parts of these functions from objective data. In the fields of irrigation, hydroelectric power, navigation, and low flow control, for instance, the financial losses caused by insufficient stream flow are an important variable. The first step in determining optimal criteria is, therefore, to derive these loss functions, which is both necessary and empirically achievable. It is also necessary to specify the forms of the individual utility of income functions, which is no small feat. However, one can make educated guesses regarding their overall form, which, if not supported by evidence from experiments, could be seen as value judgments. Not defining them solves the problem; it just leaves the answer to other, more "pragmatic" parameters' values to determine the function, which is a random process.

2.3.5 Models of Cost-benefit Analysis

Conceptually comparable models were utilized in a great deal of empirical research. We measured the income distribution effects of a Pacific Northwest project under different scenarios involving private, local, and federal development, with costs and benefits distributed among regions and income classes. First, we prepared an opportunity cost analysis of tax-raised budget money. Second, we used opportunity cost as a measure of the social cost of capital to prepare an economic analysis of Hell's Canyon project alternatives. Third, we ran a case study of the Coosa River, Alabama, to see if private development would lead to nonmarketable outputs from multipurpose projects. Lastly, we measured the income distribution effects of a Pacific Northwest project under four different scenarios. Using an objective function comparable to the one in Section 1, the fourth study aims to ascertain the distribution of costs and gains by region and income class at the federal level. There is no ranking of the options; that is left to the political procedure. But we've given you everything you need to make a call. It turns out that compared to other locations, the area receives a larger sum from federal development. A disproportionate amount of the federal costs may fall on lower income groups, contingent upon the anticipated tax revisions.

Our final piece of analysis looks at the private development plan and how it stacks up against the case study project's possible nonmarketable benefits, such flood control, and the additional costs. Actually, there are very few nonmarketable advantages offered by the private plan. You can't separate the two other probes. The opportunity cost of tax-raised funds can be determined by calculating what Musgrave termed the differential incidence of taxation, which is necessary in the case of stabilization policy that requires an offset and fiscal policy as the instrument. To cover a specific amount of spending, this amount of tax would have to be collected. To determine the tax burden, one must first determine its ultimate impact and, if that impact is on investments, one must estimate the lost rates of return. On these tax modifications, specific assumptions are made based on judgment. Customers' borrowing and saving patterns reveal the relative importance of time preferences to the value of foregone expenditure.

Consequently, the average cost of marginal tax funds is around 6%. By applying this rate to the test case of Hell's Canyon, we find that a two-dam plan outperforms the genuine private three-dam design in terms of output and cost. The public proposal's single large dam would require an additional expenditure of less than 4.5 percent under fully integrated operation. Due to the 6% opportunity cost, this increase is rejected. This approach utilizes rate-of-return comparisons, albeit it is expressed in terms of costs and benefits. This method, which takes a strict efficiency stance, uses the temporal preferences of the taxed people to determine the interest rate. If a social time preference had been used, possibly with a lower interest rate, the results would have been the same. The opportunity cost would have to be converted into a present-worth concept using the selected interest rate in order to be compared to the incremental benefit-cost ratios of the other choices. Due to its lower costs and greater benefits, the two-dam plan would have remained the preferred choice over the private plan. If we assume a 3% interest rate, the benefit-cost ratio of the missed opportunities would have been around 2.0, while the incremental investment of the large dam plan only has a ratio of 1.5. So, the results from the experiment would have been identical. To conduct this analysis, we will not assume any budget constraints.

The purpose of Hell's Canyon wasn't to select the best public works projects, but rather to evaluate and contrast various public and private landscape plans. It was a symbolic struggle between advocates of public and private power, and the additional budget monies would have been authorized if the public plan had triumphed. To be more accurate, public power initiatives would have been widely expanded. Since the public plan could have been criticized for obstructing other great public projects, using a budget constraint would have been antithetical to the situation's institutional reality. The sole repercussions were the observable benefits to downstream power, and there was no risk or uncertainty involved. Because private developers don't consider these unmarketable effects when making decisions, the designs' different advantages were primarily caused by them.

2.3.6 The Study by McKean

The theory of expenditure criteria is heavily discussed in a recent work by McKean (1961).68 Although it is similar to this paper in some respects, it takes a very different conceptual approach, and I will not attempt to summarize it all here because so much of it is concerned with saving the innocent from fallacy, outlining the basic principles of selecting criteria, and practical implementation issues. Regarding the conditions that McKean thinks are suitable, I merely give the basic outline of his reasoning. McKean emphasizes the multi-faceted nature of policy goals and the need to give merely economic efficiency-based metrics a small amount of weight. Although he emphasizes the significance of taking intangibles into account and adapting to unpredictability, his primary goal in economics is to maximize the predicted gain of real income. The end goal, according to McKean (p. 76), is to maximize the difference between the present values of the costs and benefits. He would use the marginal internal rate of return as the interest rate to derive present values. The topic of what interest rate should be employed when designing supramarginal enterprises remains unanswered, but as McKean points out, this is basically a rate of return requirement. In order for this to be the right criterion, McKean lays out the necessary assumptions. Two sets of assumptions will do: One criterion that leads to the same conclusion across the board, including benefit-cost ratios, is the assumption that funds are available without restriction at an interest rate equal to the marginal rate of return.

Both public and private investment capital are limited, and investors can reinvest their net earnings at the marginal rate of return as they accrue (p. 85). McKean elucidates the reinvestment assumption's necessity in great detail. He suggests including additional data that provide a better picture of the time profile of benefits and costs in the analysis because he is worried about how the results will be affected by the rate of return at which reinvestment happens. This is because there needs to be some arbitrariness in this matter. The profile removes the need for interest rates and forces the decision-maker, be it the president or Congress, to use his own temporal preference. But in the end, McKean does suggest the internal rate of return as the greatest easy decision-rule, acknowledging the need for such criteria. On pages 113–8, McKean argues against benefit-cost ratios. He nails the essential question: What are the program's financial limitations?

Operating and maintenance costs are funded by revenues created by benefits, including income reclaimed through taxation, according to McKean. The limitation only applies to the immediate future when investment costs are incurred. And he doesn't think it's necessary to differentiate between state and federal expenditures. And lastly, he thinks it's best to reinvest the profits. Other assumptions on these subjects have been more preferred in my own work. To begin, I anticipate that budget funds will be tight for the foreseeable future, and that operational expenses ten years from now will exert just as much pressure on these funds as present investment expenditure. Secondly, only federal expenditure should be considered a limited resource because it is the planning of a federal program that is at risk. Third, I presume there is no reinvestment. This is due, in part, to the fact that the institutional arrangements and project benefits in this area do not generate much direct revenue, and what little does not go back into the water resource field. As for the benefits that could be recovered through taxes, areas like flood control and irrigation almost never generate taxes, and it is unclear whether the taxes in power and navigation would be higher than the taxes that could have been paid by other private investments.

2.3.7 The Steiner Preemption Model

Models of this broad kind have been significantly expanded by Steiner (1959). To maximize the difference between the present value of benefits and costs, he uses the same general objective function as the models mentioned earlier. He emphasizes the need of deciding on an interest rate in order to calculate the present value of opportunity costs in addition to the benefits and expenses of initiatives. Concerning danger and uncertainty, nothing is said. His technique is unique because it uses sectoral analysis in conjunction with restrictions to highlight certain intriguing aspects of public development in a mostly private economy. According to Steiner, there are four divisions in the economy: the one receiving the budget, the one housing potential private alternatives to the public projects under consideration, the one receiving any leftover funds from the specific budget, and the one housing marginal opportunities, which would receive the private funds pushed out of the public projects. A budget limitation limits the overall expenditure for projects in sector (1). This expenditure does have some direct positive effects on sector (1), but it also has knock-on effects on the other sectors. A portion of sector (1)'s budget may go to sector (3), the broader public sector. First, there's the possibility that some capital will be redirected to sector (3) rather than sector (1) due to the lower marginal returns in the former. So, the inclusion of public sector (3) guarantees that marginal projects contribute to the public sector's overall success at the same rate as other possibilities. Second, since Steiner uses discretion, projects, and a defined budget, there is a slight chance that some money will be leftover when the projects are completed, as the total cost of the projects will not match the budget. This means that funds will flow into (3).

When the government steps in to block an investment opportunity, another consequence is a shift in the returns that private investors see on their money. According to Steiner's concept, this shifts private capital from the preemption opportunity into a marginal investment (4). The private sector suffers as a result. Steiner delves further into the scenario when opportunity costs are significant, money are drawn from the private sector, and there is no budget limit. The issue of preemption is also raised by him in this case. Combinations of budget constraints and private-public fund transfers can be absorbed by this equation, which can also reflect the losses caused by preemption of private opportunities and fully recognize opportunity costs elsewhere in the public and private sectors to the extent that this proves appropriate. In addition to the standard benefit-cost data for each project, the three opportunity costs (a1, a2, and a3) and an interest rate are the empirical magnitudes needed to execute the model.

Steiner makes no recommendations regarding the interest rate or the way the opportunity costs should be calculated. It is very challenging to empirically assign values to alternatives that would be comparable to the values linked to the projects being evaluated in the public sector, as many expenditures do not generate measurable outputs with prices. There should be no special handling of monetary costs in a market economy; they are already a measure of the private opportunity cost of marginal investments. Hell's Canyon study can all be used to determine the potential cost of private sector revenues being diverted to bolster the public budget. Thus, while the remainder of the analysis might likely be empirically applied, Steiner's focus on opportunity costs in the general public sector (sector (3)) is likely to remain a counsel of perfection.

2.4 Tinbergen's Transportation Model

In order to quantify the impact of transportation infrastructure projects on a country's GDP, Tinbergen (1956) developed a model. Production and consumption in this model take place at a number of different locations. Supply and demand equations and transportation costs between all points are calculated for each product. Every product's supply function includes the product's price as well as the prices of other products at that location. On the other hand, demand functions reflect transportation costs by include the product's delivered price. With these functions in hand, we can forecast each location's output and, by extension, its overall production and revenue. Some of the model's transportation expenses will vary due to a transportation project.

By resolving the equations with the new, reduced transportation costs in mind, we may observe how overall production and income have changed. One way to calculate the potential returns on investment in transportation projects is using this approach. It permits the effects on output that come from expanding the markets where a place's output can compete. An growth in both production and income causes demand and production to rise even further. The impact on national income is estimated to be higher by the derived estimate than by the standard benefit-cost analysis, which limits the impact to transportation cost savings. High supply elasticities indicate big increases in output, which in turn determines the extent of the discrepancy. In order to use the model as a metric for expenditure, it is necessary to do a symmetrical analysis on the cost side as well. Alternate uses of the resources would likely have knock-on impacts on revenue and production as well. Concerning interest rates and financial limitations, certain assumptions would also need to be made.

2.4.1 Chenery's SMP Model

Investment budget planning for economic development can benefit from the expenditure model put forward by H. B. Chenery (1965). Maximizing the present value of real national income, which is the result of subtracting costs from benefits, is the objective. The Social Marginal Product (SMP) is a criterion in the closed-economy model that is based on incremental ratios of present values of benefits minus operational expenses divided by the necessary increment of capital. It is a result of applying a constraint to capital funds. Individual projects are considered as steps in the program determination process, and this criterion can be used for both project design and project selection. This method is thus analogous to incremental benefit-cost ratios, with the exception that in this case, only capital expenses are included in the denominator. To meet the requirement, an interest rate is needed. In order to circumvent this problem and maintain consistent rankings, Chenery limited his criterion to projects operating in the same industry and requiring comparable amounts of capital. Additionally, Chenery extended the model to a free market economy in which the opportunity cost of foreign currency exceeds the nominal exchange rate. Two terms make up the SMP here. B—M E An equation for the entire project impact on the balance of payments (E), the premium on foreign exchange (f), the operational expenses (M), the present value of benefits (B), and the capital cost (K) is given by SMP= K. For the purpose of estimating the project's impact on the balance of payments, Chenery employs a highly nuanced repercussion analysis that takes into account the project's direct foreign exchange requirements, the import savings achieved, and the import demands resulting from the increase in national money income due to the project's multiplier effects. A number of nations use these models to inform their plans for future development.

The Programming Model by Chenery

In more recent times, Chenery and colleagues have developed overprogramming strategies to address a similar issue. The enormous possibility for empirical implementation is a practical benefit of programming. The investment allocation problem in dynamic economics can be fully solved, but only after making certain simplification assumptions to fit the linear (and nonlinear) programming apparatus. Although it might be applied to centralized economic planning in theory, the marginalist technique—which is based on Lagrangean multipliers—is essentially a partial equilibrium strategy. The use of this method to expenditure decisions typically necessitates the projection of prices, if not more.

They are more likely to be correct than prices that come out of a programming computation, and they can be made in modern economies, especially when the programs being planned are a tiny part of the economy. But in economies undergoing fast development, pricing can't be assumed because the development program itself modifies the supply and demand dynamics so strongly. In addition to solving for the total quantities, the programming technique also generates even planning prices, which must emerge from the planning computations. Rather than attempting to showcase the programming approach's outcomes, this presentation will focus on the salient features of these models, including the assumptions behind objective functions, limitations, interest rates, and other topics covered before. Chenery and Kretschmer used this model in their research on Southern Italy's development planning: Each of the 14 economic divisions represents an industry aggregate.

The input-output structure is same throughout all subsectors of a given sector, with the exception of variations in capital inputs. Using income elasticity to inform demand predictions, a set of objectives is defined, including a catalog of products. By minimizing overall investment and making the most efficient use of available labor and foreign currency, the program aims to achieve these targets. Part one of the economy's production relations is: The input-output matrix for the 14 sectors (and their subsectors) is the first thing to consider.

Each subsector is defined by one production technique using this matrix and the capital coefficients. As an alternate, you could always just buy it from another country at the current import price. There is an export demand curve for each subsector's goods that connects the amount sold to the price the good may fetch overseas. The nonlinearity introduced by this projected descending straight line foreign demand curve turns the model into a quadratic programming problem. The model, when solved, shows the optimal production in domestic subsectors in terms of demand and total output, the optimal imports and exports of different commodities, and the amount of each good. Furthermore, it discloses the total investment amount and the specific subsectors where it must be allocated. Of course, the targets can be raised if there is more funding available than is needed. This kind of model obviously has a lot of promise for cost analysis in a variety of domains. It is possible to derive the most efficient program for addressing specified needs, for instance, in water resource planning. It is also possible to estimate the most cost-effective ways of improving low-income areas while planning regional development.

2.4.2 Reinvestment and Other Models

It was the contention of Galenson and Leibenstein (1955) that decision models ought to incorporate the hitherto unconsidered consequences. One of the three main benefits they found was that some projects helped educate workers on the job. Another was that when per capita income growth was a target, the objective function had to account for the fact that different projects had different effects on population growth.

The capacity of projects to produce more capital from benefits should be taken into account, and a marginal reinvestment coefficient is proposed as a metric, in the event that the government is unable to attain an ideal level of investment. It is contended that these three consequence effects would lead to investments in urban areas' industrial initiatives being prioritized above investments in rural areas' agricultural or handicraft enterprises. To prove their claims, Galenson and Leibenstein use examples rather than a formal criterion. I aimed to formalize the decision-making process by including the reinvestment aspect in a later model. With a capital restriction in place, the objective is to maximize real national income, which is the present value of benefits minus costs. The reinvestment coefficient for each option specifies the share of gains that are put back into the system through private savings or government spending. An efficiency term that shows the present value of benefit minus operating cost per marginal dollar of investment and a term that prioritizes the output portion to be reinvested make up the two parts of the resulting criterion. This premium needs to be generated by the return on investment of the capital that can be reinvested. This is relevant to the analysis of the planner's time preference that was worked out in Section 3 above; the resultant criterion is particularly sensitive to the choice of interest rate due to the lengthy perspective overtime.

Development Model proposed by A.K. Sen

Sen(1957) put out a number of theoretical models to show how a developing nation's development strategy is problematic. These models are more for theoretical purposes than actual planning; their purpose is to give empirically feasible rules of thumb. When considering potential reinvestment levels and balance-of-payments impacts, Sen is especially curious about the optimal level of capital intensity for development. For a developing nation, he constructs a basic sectoral model and uses it to assess potential development approaches. In one section of the economy, there is a backward sector with high unemployment and infinite supply of labor; in the other, there is an advanced sector with two divisions, one making capital goods and the other "corn." There are two ways to increase the output of "corn," one that uses less capital and has poor labor productivity and the other that uses more capital but has greater productivity.

All salaries are spent, and any surplus is reinvested, according to Ricardo. Choosing the strategy that generates the largest surplus is essential for optimizing the rate of growth, which is defined as the rate of reinvestment per dollar of original investment. A higher rate of surplus per unit of output is possible with the capital-intensive technique since labor productivity is increased. However, the return on investment will be lower.

Is the additional surplus per worker, made possible by the more capital intensive technique, enough to compensate for the total surplus loss due to the smaller output caused by sinking capital into intensive uses? This is the empirical question that can only be answered by obtaining magnitudes for the model's parameters. Sen incorporates international trade into this strategy in a second model. He thinks that the capital-intensive method necessitates the purchase of foreign machinery, which can be funded by selling part of the maize that is being grown. To get the reinvestible surplus, we need to maximize the rate of corn surplus, which includes not only the corn that goes into wages but also the corn that is absorbed by exports.

Maximizing the rate of growth of output is a strange and unclear goal function in real-world scenarios with different temporal profiles. On the other hand, until a change in methodology occurs, the growth rate stays constant in Sen's model assuming the parameters stay the same. Therefore, faster growth will always outweigh output losses in the near run, provided the target date is set far enough in the future. According to Sen, maximizing the rate of growth is an extreme example that just takes into account the economic situation at a distant moment in time. The second extreme scenario, according to Sen, is basic turnover criterion, which ignores all but the first period.

A "recovery" period is used by Sen to reintroduce time discount into the analysis. There must be a certain number of years where the production of the two methods is equal if the capital-intensive technique does, in fact, create less output in the beginning but more in the end (the one scenario where a genuine choice problem exists). Governments can choose between capital-intensive techniques by comparing their "recovery" periods with the number of years of output they want to include in their target functions. Analysts can incorporate key factual characteristics of developing nations into their work with the help of these models. The practical assessment of Sen's proposed models could be useful, especially when big strategic decisions are at stake, such focusing on city industries or small businesses in rural areas. But I think overprogramming techniques can do everything these explicit sectoral models can, and more, because they drastically simplify reality to keep the mathematics from getting out of hand.

2.5 Summary

Hence we observe that maximization of utility is the basic principle of taxation so that it assists in economic growth. There are several models to learn from like the A.K. Sen model, Chenery model, Tinbergen's model that each researcher and thinker came up with their own innovative methods to manage investments and reinvestments for the welfare of the country. There are, however, several questions related to welfare and whether the government can play a role in controlling the market forces or can simply work to provide a healthy 'financial scenario' to the citizens for the purpose of economic welfare.

Chapter III

Methodology

3.1 Overview of Research Problem

Preliminary research shows that previous studies in India have mostly concentrated on trying to establish a connection between the country's tax system and its GDP development. Research shows that state economies feel the pinch of income and commodity-service taxes, but feel the full force of property and capital transaction taxes. Lowering income taxes should be the primary goal of policymakers. Additionally, it was discovered that some areas and states are considering modifying their tax systems to entice businesses or encourage growth. The World Tax Index also indicated that, in terms of the effect of taxes on GDP growth, personal income taxes, corporation taxes, social security contributions, and value-added taxes are in that order of severity. In order to enhance capital creation in the country, previous studies have failed to provide a thorough and organized framework for comprehending the investment opportunities presented by income tax law.

3.2 Operationalization of Theoretical Constructs

Quantitative, mixed-method, and qualitative approaches are the most common in domain research, while there are many more. Researchers in quantitative fields utilize estimates to look for differences or variable relations in order to answer queries regarding correlations among variables (Bilgin, 2017), as stated in Koys and Adams (2015) and Saunders et al. (2015).

Saunders et al. (2018) noted that mixed-method systems incorporate qualities of both qualitative and quantitative methodologies. Researchers favor a qualitative approach when trying to make sense of the specific phenomenon (Silverman 2016). However, neither the quantitative nor the mixed methods were sufficient for this investigation, since the former focuses on the examination of correlations and similarities between variables, while the latter seeks to test hypotheses and take causative effects into account.

Statistical significance or insignificance calculations are not part of this study (Saunders et al., 2018). Leadership perspective on the development of job satisfaction for business performance is explored in this study through a qualitative case technique that employs in-depth interviews with study participants. To confirm the work, boost the credibility of the research findings, and help overcome all inherent biases coming from the use of a single method, all of the data obtained will be triangulated utilizing a triangulation strategy (Johnson et al., 2017).

3.3 Research Purpose and Questions

Here are the primary areas of inquiry:

- RQ1: How does direct taxes affect market growth?

- RQ2: How does indirect taxation affect economic growth?

Thirdly, how does the Goods and Services Tax (GST) affect the amount of money the government gets in taxes?

- RQ3: How do investments, startups, and taxes affect the growth of businesses in a country?

- RQ4: What effect do these types of taxes have on the expansion of the national economy?

By posing these questions, researchers are able to fill in knowledge gaps and get to the bottom of pressing policy and development concerns.

Hypothesis

> According to the study's hypothesis, a country's economic progress is positively impacted by higher taxes.

Economic development is the dependent variable while "taxation" is the independent variable in this study. In order to facilitate discussions at the conclusion of the study, the variables have been identified and laid out clearly. The study examines various scenarios in which the country's economic development varies in response to the policies and types of taxes in place.

3.4 Research Design

The study will employ both quantitative and qualitative methods to examine reports and literature in order to address the research topics that have been proposed. To investigate the function of taxes and its impact on the country's economic growth, the research will employ a case study methodology based on semi-structured in-depth interviews (Saunders et al., 2018).

Notably, this study did not pursue or aim to use other designs, such as phenomenological, grounded theory, ethnographic, or correlational designs; these alternatives might have been more appropriate. Finding or demonstrating a relationship between many variables (independent and dependent variables) is the goal of an objective research study. For a better grasp of people's motivations and perspectives, qualitative research is the way to go (Silverman, 2016). In order to acquire insight into the topic of taxation and development, the researcher must ask participants to answer open-ended semi-structured interview questions. This will allow them to assess the influence and effect of different forms of taxation. Further, as stated by Saunders et al. (2018), qualitative analysis has the potential to provide light on a problem or aid in the development of ideas that can be tested in a subsequent quantitative investigation. The investigation will benefit from the formation of correlations.

To better understand how governments in both developed and developing nations promote economic development through public spending and public financing, as well as why some good government strategies fail, this study will employ semi-structured interviews to probe the "why and why not" of people's reactions to growth and taxes.

In addition, studies will be able to include a wider range of viewpoints and methods in their analyses, which will improve our knowledge of the nation's issues and how to address them.

In order to help validate the study's trustworthiness, the researchers used a triangulation approach. In order to make the research findings more credible and legitimate, researchers apply the triangulation methodology (Cohen 2000). Using a range of approaches, triangulation helps explain and explore complex human behavior in a more balanced way, which benefits readers of the study (Murdock 2019).

3.5 Population and Sample Selection

Present and past employees of the Indian government's taxation department exemplified the study's population. The study's goal could not have been accomplished without using purposive sampling. Researchers employ their best judgment in purposeful sampling to select respondents who are most likely to give accurate and relevant information in order to answer research questions and achieve study objectives (Abdullah et al. 2017).

Purposive sampling allowed for the selection of fifteen (15) study participants who fulfilled all criteria. Researchers employ their best judgment to choose study participants using purposeful sampling, a non-probability sampling method (Yin, 2018).

The tax officers' roles, classifications, and the total number of rules and regulations are detailed in the following sample population.

The interview was conducted after obtaining permission from the research participants. Those who were chosen for the study had to have worked for the government and had direct experience with taxing responsibilities. Under the next section of the study, we detail how the participants were chosen.

3.6 Participant Selection

As India continues to expand economically, it is crucial to base fifteen semi-structured interview questions around this topic. Interviewees can feel safe answering questions honestly because the information will remain confidential. To find out what government officials need to know about economic development and loopholes, we will conduct semi-structured interviews with taxation officers. Before the interview, we emailed them to ask for their permission to go ahead and do it. After I heard back from the participant that they were interested in taking part in the study, I drafted up an informed consent form and sent them a letter inviting them to a time and place that would work for them.

In order to get enough information from the 25 respondents for a qualitative case study, Tong and Dew (2016) said that the researcher should prioritize choosing people whose opinions are relevant to the research subject.

According to Morse (2015), the research phenomenon will only become clearer and easier to grasp once the data saturation point is achieved. All overlapping information has the ability to remove the unknown problems, and any variables that, if understood, would change the study's outcomes (ibid). As a first step in conducting interviews, he said, pick a small sample and keep going until you run out of topics or data.

According to Sivell et al. (2019), it is important for the researcher to conduct interviews in a comfortable environment so that the interviewee feels at ease enough to speak up. The researcher also needs to be accommodating and thorough when it comes to providing research participants with convenient locations and timing so that the study interviews may take place when and where the tax authorities are most available.

The researcher still runs the risk of excluding a high-quality sample from the collection and thus failing to obtain all of the data needed to answer the research questions, even when they employ deliberate sampling (ibid). But these people were chosen for the study on purpose; they know the government's tax system, public spending role, and overall organization inside and out.

3.7 Instrumentation

Content analysis

Collecting data entails getting the meat and potatoes of the phenomenon under research, which means keeping an eye on how the participants are feeling and thinking (Silverman, 2016). The information was retrieved using both primary and secondary sources. In order to gain a broad picture of the taxation structure, regulations, limits, and limitations that go into deciding government initiatives, the study relied on semi-structured interviews as its main data source. Primary data came from in-depth, one-on-one interviews and participant observation. Articles from scholarly journals, official government websites, and other sources were combed through using the secondary method. Because of this, the researcher was able to zero in on the issue at hand and stop wasting time perusing irrelevant literature. Specifically, the content analysis study was helpful in that regard.

In order to obtain in-depth insight and information from study participants, semi-structured interviews allow the researcher to concentrate, provide framework, and give the flexibility the participants need to speak freely and clarify answers with follow-up questions (Shirani, 2015). The researcher is able to learn about the officials' backgrounds and experiences through interviews, and then interpret and apply their findings (Yin 2018).

Establishing rapport with the respondent and obtaining the necessary support to gather reliable data for validation are two other important benefits of doing the interview one-on-one. According to Yin (2018), six types of evidence can be used in qualitative research: interviews, documentation, direct observation, physical artifacts, participant observation, and archival records. Furthermore, there is also the possibility of using a combination of these methods. Interviews, first-hand observations, and document analysis (including content analysis) are the main sources of evidence used in the study. Researchers rely on document analysis because it allows them to compile relevant materials that shed light on the topic under study (Schneider, 2016).

The original text was useful in elucidating the government's financial management practices. In addition, the study combed through government websites, journals from the Ministry of Finance's archives, and policy documents pertaining to taxation and spending. An integral aspect of methodological triangulation is the utilization of several evidence sources, including interviews, record analysis, and observation (Oesterreich and Teuteberg 2016; Yin 2018).

In order to ensure that the data was reliable and consistent, the study employed a methodological strategy known as methodological triangulation, drawing from the aforementioned sources. By combining data from many sources, including research interviews, documents retrieved from literature reviews, and first-hand observations made both before and after data collection, methodological triangulation increases the reliability and depth of a study.

In order to maintain its credibility throughout, the study followed the methods outlined by Hunter et al. (2015). Keeping in mind the characteristics of power dynamics inside the interview, observing textual signals, and evaluating the ongoing process were all factors in the study's consideration of previous interviews and experiences.

Researchers could attain reliability and generalizability, according to Morse (2015), by using member checking.

To ensure the study's validity, we digitally recorded the interviews and stored the recordings in a secure location to protect the interviewees' confidentiality, in accordance with the University's ethical standards. We also used the signed consent form to reduce the possibility of bias.

3.8 Data Collection Procedures

In order to establish trust and get reliable data, the interviewers adhered to the protocol and kept the interviewees in a safe environment before, during, and after the interview. You can find the interview protocol in Appendix B. The researcher met with a small group of interviewees at a central location for identification and started the interview by thanking them and providing a brief overview of the study's topic. Every person was given a signed copy of the consent form, which I then distributed. To make sure the data is consistent, we reminded the interviewees to use a mobile device or laptop to record the interview and to follow the member verification method.

The researcher outlines how they performed the interviews with the research participants in the appendix of the paper. The interviews lasted about 30 to 50 minutes. Bauman (2015) and Bowden & Galindo-Gonzalez (2015) argued that researchers should give participants complete disclosure of the interview process to assure compliance and to get a detailed summary of their experiences. The major technique of data collecting for qualitative case study analysis also involves interviewing participants. According to Hancock and Algozzine (2017), researchers are able to get into the respondents' extensive personal knowledge through case study interviews.

If there aren't enough people taking part in the study, it might not be able to collect enough data to answer the research question. As part of the standardization process for sample size, it is imperative that all respondents adhere to the same format and method when answering the questions, and that the investigator applies the same standard when interpreting the answers (Malterud et al. 2015).

Researchers can learn more about the people they interview and, ideally, get to the bottom of their experiences by conducting in-depth interviews (Granot & Greene, 2015). An important benefit of using semi-structured interviews with free-form questions was that it allowed us to go deeper into the participants' real-life experiences, which is an important point to emphasize.

Lastly, the study collected data and made sure that members had controls to prove that the data was legitimate and accurate, so that there wouldn't be any problems with the documents being changed and losing their literal meaning or with any breaches of confidentiality. In order to guarantee the study's reliability and generalizability, the researcher made every effort to obtain and use documents that were relevant to the study during the last five years, as per Yin (2018), who states that data gathering instruments must be explicit.

3.8.1 Data Management

First, data management; second, preserving data in journals; third, entering data into CAQDAS; fourth, analyzing researcher notes across the study; and lastly, storing all data on an external storage device were the five stages outlined by Yin (2018) for organizing and securing information. The use of cellphones and laptop applications was approved by all participants in this study.

The researcher utilized technology as the main tool and exercised freedom in data deployment to organize the data. Coding, transcribing, interpreting, and summarizing all data was done using research software like Microsoft Word and Excel.

3.9 Data Analysis

According to Yin (2018), the researcher acts as a data collector in qualitative research. Purposive sampling is employed in the study. Direct, one-on-one interactions between research participants and interviewers using semi-structured and open-ended questions will yield the necessary data. Triangulated data will be derived from all sources, including interviews, records, and direct observation.

Research that employs multiple perspectives on the same event (e.g., interviews, reports, and observations) is known as triangulation, according to Fusch and Ness (2015). To help validate the study's findings, they're utilizing triangulation. Triangulation is a method for finding trends by comparing the interview data with that from secondary sources and comparing the transcripts to one another. A matrix was generated for each interviewee in the study so that themes and connections could be easily identified. The interviewee's interpretation of the data gathered during the short session was checked using a member check to ensure accuracy.

The researcher can confirm the validity, interpretation, and understanding of the respondent's comments through a two-way analysis and interpretation, which is a key method for getting positive input from the interviewee (Merriam and Tisdell, 2015).

No changes were necessary during the member checking process, and the interviewee was provided with a copy of the research explanations.

We used Microsoft Word to code, arrange, and transcribe the audio and documents in order to get versatility, which is essential for recognizing nodes and matrices. This allowed us to find the study topics that were relevant to our research objectives. I idealized influence, (ii) inspiring motivation, (iii) intellectual stimulation, and (iv) personalized consideration are the four pillars of transformational leadership theory that were compared to the study's topics.

In order to get a good grasp on the tactics for public expenditure on economic growth in India, the research topics were linked to the many aspects of the theoretical framework.

Reliability and Validity of the Study

Reliability

The degree to which the results would remain unchanged if the analysis were to be repeated is what we mean when we talk about reliability. Various perspectives on the significance of the analysis should be utilized by qualitative researchers, according to Fusch and Ness (2015). In order to assure data consistency, strength, and dependability, the study zeroed in on all the modifications impacting the analysis technique to make sure data is compatible. Throughout the interview process, participants were provided with clear and understandable questions, a transcript of the interview, and a copy of the transcript for their records.

Yin (2018) asserts that member verification, rather than transcript analysis, will guarantee the veracity of the acquired data. Furthermore, Fusch and Ness (2015) proposed that qualitative researchers employ member checking in interview validation to bolster evidence, and they also noted that member checking enhanced the study's reliability.

Respondents were satisfied since the researcher gave them enough of time to finish member verification and gave them copies of the interpretations to make sure they were accurate. Rechecks of members and assessments of transcripts demonstrate the trustworthiness of the study.

Validity

Trustworthiness of research results depends on researcher following research standards, which include principles of reliability, transferability, and honesty. If the research's validity is compromised while it is being conducted, the quality of the research will be compromised, according to Yin (2018). In order to ensure that the data is accurately interpreted in order to reach valid findings, validity is the primary metric of research quality.

According to Proctor (2017), in order to guarantee the validity and reliability of the study results, qualitative researchers must adjust their conclusions in light of the fact that their data is subjective, interpretive, and contextual. Therefore, for the research to be valuable to readers and other academics, the results need to be consistent, credible, applicable, and convincing. Once again, scholars should consider the key elements of conformability, reliability, transferability, and integrity to ensure their work withstands scrutiny. Instead of focusing on data quantity, the analysis should aim for data accuracy, richness, and reliability (Proctor, 2017).

By comparing and contrasting different interpretations of the data with research participants, triangulation guarantees accuracy from multiple angles. Constant engagement, external job audits, and member checks all contributed to the study's legitimacy by ensuring that the data analysis was accurate.

According to Proctor (2017), in order for a study to be considered transferable, the researcher has to make sure that the results may be applied to different settings. Careful explanation of the analysis context was provided in the report to assist readers in appropriately applying the results to varied scenarios.

The study meticulously documented any irregularities or unexpected occurrences in order to provide a clearer understanding of the results and aid future researchers in their quest to duplicate them with confidence. By remaining impartial throughout analysis and disregarding the biases of the research participants, the study further ensured compliance.

According to Malterud et al. (2015), respondents should make sure to answer the research questions completely to avoid risking data saturation. The study's standardization of the sample size allowed it to reach saturation with ten (10) taxation officials. By following a predetermined framework, respondents can consistently answer the same questions, and the researcher can rest assured that their interpretation will be consistent as well.

3.10 Research Design Limitation

In order to validate the study, Yin (2018) defined assumptions as truths that have not been validated yet. As a result, a number of assumptions were made by the researcher throughout the research design development and analysis processes.

Additionally, the researcher made the assumption that the tiny sample population is representative of all revenue authorities in India. In addition, the tax officials' opinions might be prejudiced and skewed towards or against the government, thus it's hard to assume that they answered interview questions truthfully and properly. Additionally, the researcher assumed that all participants would be well-versed in effective techniques to boost the country's overall development. Finally, the study's lack of generalizability and the possibility that participants may be reluctant to disclose personal information openly constitute limits that constitute a critical flaw in the research design.

3.11 Conclusion

In this chapter, we covered the steps involved in doing a qualitative analysis, as well as why a qualitative case study was essential for delving into the country's tax paperwork and officials' replies. This chapter provided an overview of the research strategy, methodology, and sample size for the case study that examined the strategies employed by taxation officials to enhance the government's involvement in expenditure. In order to answer the research question, the study also highlighted the value of developing themes for data analysis and comparing them to the relevant literature and conceptual framework. The study emphasized the significance of triangulation and member verification in ensuring reliability and validity. Results can help tax officials increase government collection and spend money more discretely. Insights gained from this case study may provide light on how taxes play a part in guiding India's economic development and progress through the control of public and governmental spending.

The research on the role of tax authorities and government spending in fostering economic development of the country is introduced in the next chapter.

Chapter IV

Results

4.1 Introduction

The study's significance in applying triangulation approach to validate the research findings is emphasized in Chapter 3, which also covers the chosen methodology, design, and data collecting for the research. The results obtained from the study's participants are detailed in this section. Interviews and direct participant observation provided the data.

Additionally, the results were consistent with the study's literature in answering the research questions. How does taxation affect a nation's economic development? This was the main research question for the qualitative case study. The researcher interviewed fifteen Indian tax officials and lawyers with a combined forty years of experience in the field via semi-structured online interviews in order to get a satisfactory answer to the topic.

In order to bolster the data and provide more accurate conclusions, the researcher utilized a qualitative multiple case study.

Thematic analysis was used to consolidate the study's qualitative data. We looked at the overarching themes that came out as the participants discussed the research topics. In order to verify the veracity of their responses, the interviews were imported into Excel and then converted to Word documents.

Additionally, the results presented in this chapter addressed some of the primary study questions posed to the respondents. The inductive examination of the qualitative data that flowed via this part follows. As the research progresses, these themes and patterns regarding the thinking and tactics used by tax officials to aid the government become apparent.

Main Point 1: Good Tax Revenue from GST

Second Theme: The Significance of India's Economic Growth and Development

Thirdly, the effects and consequences of taxes on economic development. Fourthly, the role of public expenditure in enhancing economic development. Fifthly, the Indian government's tax strategy.

Review of the budget for 2024–25, a crucial document released by the Indian government in January of 2024, is also covered in this chapter along with the findings from its content analysis. Public spending and tax policies enacted by the Indian government (GoI) under several headings are discussed in depth in a report titled "The Indian Economy" that was released by the Department of Economic Affairs of the Ministry of Finance. The report's content analysis mostly covers the following topics:

First Topic: How Often Is "Direct Taxation" Mentioned in Articles About India's Economy

The second theme is the prevalence of coverage of "indirect taxes" in the Indian economy.

Third Topic: Separate Examinions of "Taxation" in India's Federal Budget

The fourth theme is the role of "development" in India's economy. The fifth theme covers the several main sorts of taxes.

Theme 6: Central topics covered in various portions of the developmental coding

Seventh Theme: Taxation's Effect on Economic Growth

Following this, we delved further into these topics.

4.2 The demographic information

Only tax officials in the sixty- to seventy-year-old age range were contacted for the qualitative case studies. All of the respondents had a common educational background and were recruited for the position of tax officer in a competitive examination run by the government of India, so there was a lot of demographic consistency. They have collaborated closely with the state governments and, subsequently, India, and have worked tirelessly. They are well-versed in the ins and outs of government spending policies.

4.3 Results

4.3.1 How is Goods and Services Tax (GST) a good form of tax collection and revenue?

A reduction in the number of tax rates and the elimination of several tax types is the primary finding of the data analysis.

Thirteen people polled said it made things more transparent, decreased the amount of indirect taxes, and actually enhanced compliance and revenue collection. Because it eliminates the domino effect of input taxes, it is an improved kind of indirect taxation. Better tax collection is the result of increased business activity.

A national tax on the production, distribution, and purchase of goods and services is known as the Goods and Services Tax (GST), according to Shaik et al. (2015). The Goods and Services Tax (GST), one of India's most significant tax reforms, is about to bring together the economies of the many states and increase GDP. There are a plethora of indirect taxes that firms and businesses are currently required to pay, including VAT, service tax, sales tax, entertainment tax, octroi, and luxury tax. All of these taxes would disappear if GST is put into place. There would be just one national tax, and it would be overseen by the federal government. Another distinction is that GST is not applied during production but rather at the moment of consumption, making it distinct from other taxes.

Five people who took the survey think that tax policies are significant because of the effect they have on economic justice and efficiency. A well-designed tax system should aim to raise enough money to pay for essential public services and new infrastructure while simultaneously considering concerns about income inequality. The Abbreviation for "Goods and Services Tax" is GST. All goods and services, with a few exceptions, will be subject to this domestic trade tax, which is structured like a value-added tax. All inputs, including capital items, are free from a value added tax. Therefore, it amounts to a broad tax on consumption within the country. A tax on consumption in this form is both practical and economical. A proportional tax on consumption would result from a flat rate and minimal exemptions. The tax should be levied according to the principle of destination, which states that the tax on a good should go to the state where the consumer resides. This way, the tax burden can be dispersed according to consumption. If there is just a single level of taxation in the state, or if the tax is only imposed at the federal level, then this is what happens automatically. The implementation of a goods and services tax (GST) at both the federal and state levels presents unique challenges for federations.

More extensive and greater coverage of input tax set-off and service tax set-off, consolidation of numerous taxes under the GST, and the eventual elimination of CST are all anticipated to provide additional relief to industry, trade, agriculture, and consumers as a result of GST implementation at the federal and state levels. Industry and trade have both responded positively. Because of this, we should not pass up the chance to implement GST now, while conditions are favorable and the economy is growing steadily with only moderate inflation, because it provides us with the finest choice to expand our tax base.

In his 2014 study, Saravanan Venkadasalam used the Least Squares Dummy Variable Model (LSDVM) to examine how the Goods and Services Tax (GST) affected the GDP growth of ASEAN member states. Seven out of ten ASEAN nations are reportedly using the GST already, according to him. He went on to say that, in line with expectations and economic theory, final consumption expenditures at the household and government level are positively and strongly related to GDP. However, countries' experiences with the post-GST era are diverse. Both Thailand and the Philippines have a strong inverse correlation with the rate of national development. At the same time, Singapore demonstrates a strong positive correlation. Without a doubt, countries that implement GST invariably see growth. But governance, compliance cost, and economic distortion all play a role in how big of an effect there will be. The success of the Goods and Services Tax (GST) hinges on its impartial and reasonable design, which should be straightforward, easy to understand, and greatly improve involuntary compliance. The costs should be accurate and not based on assumptions. A system of audits would be put in place to ensure compliance.

Similar to value-added tax, the GST system uses a preexisting idea. Here, the GST imposed at the moment of sale can be offset against taxes paid at a lower level. Here are a few features of the GST model:

Central Goods and Services Tax and State Goods and Services Tax are the two parts that make up Goods and Services Tax (GST). All goods and services sold or given in India would be subject to GST, with the exception of a few items that are specifically exempted. Central and state governments will collect and remit GST at different rates. Central Goods and Service Tax is the sole tax for which the input tax credit facility will be available at the federal level. Put another way, you can't use the input tax credit (ITC) from the Central Goods and Service tax to offset the State Goods and Service tax, and vice versa.

The country's complex taxation system is anticipated to be profoundly affected by the Goods and Service Tax (GST) bill. It will probably reduce inflation and enhance the tax to GDP ratio of the country. The services sector may find things more challenging as a result of the reform, while the manufacturing sector stands to gain. Even if a 1% to 2% increase in GDP growth is anticipated, the outcomes will not be analyzed until the GST is put into place. All throughout the globe, people are reacting differently. Following the implementation of the GST, the GDP growth rates of New Zealand, Canada, Australia, and Thailand were all lower than expected. The proposed 1% tax, which is meant to make the states happy by making up for the money they lost from the interstate CST, will probably backfire. In all likelihood, it might have a negative impact on GDP. A 1% tax has already met with opposition in Congress. You can presume that the GS Tax rate, which is anticipated to be about 17-18%, will have no effect on your tax liability. Government coffers will not be bolstered by this tax rate. The manufacturing sector, which currently pays a tax rate of about 24%, will benefit from the rate. The fast-moving consumer goods (FMCG), automotive (auto), and cement (cement) industries stand to gain the most. This is because a tax rate of

24% to 38% is presently putting a strain on their finances. The services sector is the one that will take a hit. Starting on June 1st of this year, there was an increase of 12–14%. They will be unable to withstand an additional 4% hike. There shouldn't be any difference between the products and services sectors as a result of the consistency in the taxes rate. If the government proposes a higher GS Tax rate, say 20% or 24%, no one has considered what effect it will have on the service industry. The tax-to-GDP ratio will undoubtedly rise with a higher GST rate, and the government will have more financial clout to increase capital expenditure. In all likelihood, this will cause the economy to expand. The whole exercise does have one positive aspect. Under the GST law, the unorganized sector—which has a cost advantage equal to the taxes rate—could be subjected. Many haphazard businesses in industries like electrical, paints, hardware, etc., will finally be subject to taxes because of this. The saying is easier than the doing. Implementing the GST reform in a way that brings the unorganized sector into its purview will require extensive and careful preparation. Two things will happen as a result: first, the tax base will grow, and second, the organized players will gain back some of the money they're losing to the unorganized sector. During parliamentary sessions, there are still many unexplored areas that need to be investigated. Without negatively impacting any industry, this will restore integrity to the taxation system.

Attention All Individuals and Businesses – Companies stand to gain from higher consumption and lower prices as a result of the proposed point-of-sale collection of both federal and state taxes. This is because both components would be charged to manufacturing costs.

Indirect taxation a good tool of revenue collection

Revenues in Nigeria have been distributed in accordance with the formula proposed by Ad-hoc Fiscal Commissions or a principle selected by the government. Thirteen revenue allocation Commissions have been established since 1946 (Taiwo, 2008). The Commissions' recommendations for a revenue sharing formula varied in accordance with the government's economic fortunes and goals. Even more importantly, taxes is the primary means by which the government acquires the funds necessary to pay for its programs and to exert its influence over other sectors of the economy. Furthermore, various forms of resistance, such as evasion, avoidance, and other corrupt practices, can easily be perpetuated within the direct taxes bracket, making tax revenue mobilization a difficult issue to address in less developed economies when it comes to funding developmental activities. Seen as economic sabotage, these actions are often cited as the cause of the country's lack of progress.

All nations, regardless of ideology or political system, collect taxes so that non-revenue producing services like infrastructure, education, health, communications, employment, and essential public services like maintaining law and order can be efficiently and continuously expanded. Taxation itself has far-reaching positive implications on encouraging more effective and transparent governance.

In addition to macro effects on capacity output, employment, pricing, and growth, micro effects on income distribution and resource efficiency are also part of tax's economic impact, according to Akhor (2014). Because of the declining level of income generation, less developed countries cannot rely on taxes as a tool to promote economic growth. Therefore, macroeconomic stability has been achieved or influenced by the use of adjusting or fine-tuning tax rates. Nations like Canada, the US, the Netherlands, and the UK have shown how governments may use tax income to shape economic growth. They have used the money they get from VAT and import duties to build a prosperous economy (Oluba, 2008). Natural resource taxes contribute significantly to Africa's overall tax revenue increase. Pfister (2009) listed royalties, production sharing, and the oil and mining industry's corporate income tax as sources of this income. Crude oil is the principal export of the emerging nation of Nigeria. Natural gas, coal, limestone, lead, zinc, iron ore, tin, and other natural resources are also abundant. A nation's economic growth and development may be hindered if it relies too much on direct tax revenue, according to most economists, particularly development and international economists (Okafor, 2012). This is because direct tax revenue is vulnerable to fluctuations in oil prices and CIT, and because tax evasion and avoidance are common and easy to implement.

Theme two: Economic growth and development of India and its meaning

According to twelve respondents, the government's tax policies must be working if more and more low-income people are getting out of poverty. In terms of development, India possesses enormous potential and resources. India is heading in the right path with the proper policies and environment. Boost to the national economy, which in turn improves living conditions for the populace. Economic progress should disproportionately benefit lower-class citizens.

Social actors have permeated the Indian state more than many East and Southeast Asian states, according to Mukherji and Jha (2023). India, in contrast to China, could not embrace globalization with the same zeal or outlaw private entrepreneurship. Any form of state-driven globalization or full-scale nationalization would necessitate the state, which would then have far more influence over groups like farmers, industrialists, and unions. Building a social consensus on policies that promote economic growth and development in India required time for those policies to evolve. In this development model, the state and society work together, with social actors serving to limit the state's power, even during its most dominant periods. Within the state, there was a dispute over developmental concepts. To make significant changes to economic policy, we must go back in time and follow a pattern of incremental shifts in thinking and action, with economic crises serving as occasional checkpoints. This study argues that this dynamic is fundamental to comprehending India's globalization beyond the green revolution and its political implications, including the country's food grain self-sufficiency. The plot revolves around achieving higher rates of economic growth through a series of intermediate steps following the establishment of a policy consensus among various stakeholders. Recent economic downturns hastened the formation of a new agreement. In the years following 2003, India's growth rates started to resemble those of China. In India, when the economy was restricted and heavily regulated, GDP expanded by 3 to 4 percent annually from 1956 to 1974.

According to Pradhan et al. (2021), digital financial systems have arisen as a result of rising growth and convergence of financial and ICT platforms. These systems have created new chances to reduce wealth disparities in emerging nations. This article takes a look at 20 Indian states from 1991 to 2018 and analyses the long-term and short-term relationships between GDP growth, financial inclusion programs, and information and communication technology infrastructure development. In both the short and long run, we demonstrate substantial temporal causality between these variables using the Granger-causality technique. Our data shows that these Indian states can't succeed economically unless they carefully coordinate the expansion of their information and communication technology (ICT) infrastructure with their plans to increase financial inclusion and boost economic growth.

They believe that higher economic growth for the country can only be achieved through sustainable development. They argue that, as seen in the chart below, financial inclusion and ICT structures contribute to higher economic growth.

Figure 3: Economic growth
Source: **Self (as modified from Pradhan et al, 2021)**

Theme three: Impact and effect of taxation on economic development

More people participating in direct taxation would lead to more economic development, according to thirteen respondents. One way the wealthy can help fund the country's progress is through direct taxes. Demand for goods and services is affected by direct taxes since these levies reduce the buying power of customers. Production and economic growth are both hit hard when demand takes a nosedive. Thus, the tax rate ought not to be very high. Indirect taxes have a multiplier effect on economic growth as businesses and industries expand. Businesses will do better if GST and other indirect taxes are increased. Startups are great for the economy because they gradually bring more money into the government coffers. The startup scene is ripe with opportunities for young entrepreneurs. In this area, they are a breath of fresh air.

According to Srivastava et al. (2010), tax revenue is essential for the expansion of the Indian economy. The three-tiered federal structure in India, which includes the Union Government, the State Governments, and the Urban/Rural Local Bodies, is accompanied with a sophisticated tax system. As per the Indian Constitution, the authority to collect taxes and duties is divided among the three levels of government. Over the past few decades, the Indian government has worked to overhaul the country's tax laws, and its reform efforts have paid off handsomely. The tax-to-GDP ratio for the center rose from 9.2% in 2003–04 to 11.5% in 2008–09. An increase in direct taxes is largely responsible for the rise in tax collections that has been observed during the past five years. For this study, we used tax revenue as a percentage of GDP and tax revenue collected by the central government for the five consecutive fiscal years, from 2002-03 to 2007-08. Our goals were to look at how tax revenue affected India's GDP and how changes in taxation affected tax revenue. According to the Indian Economic Survey Report 2008-09, the data was harvested. In spite of the economic downturn in India, we discovered that the central government's tax GDP per cent climbed 46% in the fiscal year 2008-09 (BE) from a low of 6.5% in the fiscal year 2002-03, and that tax income from both direct and indirect sources has been steadily rising. It is reasonable to assume that India's gross domestic product and tax income have been positively affected by the recent changes and innovations in direct and indirect taxes.

The relationship between taxes and growth is a long-standing topic of debate in economics, according to Neog (2018). The rate of economic growth is unrelated to taxation. On the other hand, taxation can sway people's spending habits, which in turn affects GDP growth. The opposite is true for tax revenue, which is a significant source of funds for any government. Markets, consumer habits, and investment choices can be impacted by adaptive and reasonable expectations about changes in tax laws. The connection between taxes and economic expansion has also been the subject of a great deal of study. In their study, Martin and Fardmaneshi (1990) used a restricted variant of the model and cross-sectional data from 76 industrialized and developing nations between 1972 and 1981 to examine the effects of taxation, spending, and deficits. Reducing deficits through tax and expenditure reduction led to growth, while deficits themselves were contractionary. For Malaysia, researchers looked at how GDP growth affected tax receipts. Any nation's economic growth has been impeded by the improper distribution of resources. This study's findings demonstrate a one-way correlation between GDP growth and total tax revenue, with a short-run adjustment speed of 21%. A growth proxy was GDP, while explanatory variables were direct and indirect tax receipts. According to the study by Gale and Samwick (2015), there is no consistent relationship between tax collections or top income tax rates and employment or economic growth. The dependent variable here is the real personal income per capita. The variables that were used for analysis were state as a dummy variable, total tax revenues as a percentage of personal income, productive investments, and social spending. The impact of indirect tax collections on GDP growth in Nigeria was examined by Akhor and Ekundayo (2016). Revenue from value-added taxes (VAT), customs and excise duties, and overall economic growth (GDP) were considered independent variables. There is a strong and negative correlation between value-added tax and actual GDP.

The effect of customs and excise charge on Nigeria's real GDP was negative, but not statistically significant. In India, a comparable study was carried out.

4.3.2 Hypotheses

> ➤ The study hypothesizes that greater taxation leads to better and a positive economic development of the country

Theme 4: Improvement of economic development through public expenditure

Up until the 20th century, the state could only do so much. Consequently, government spending was not prioritized over government earnings. It was considered undesirable that the revenue increased beyond what was necessary to cover the cost on preserving law and order. Many people's views on the role of government have evolved in recent decades. We are currently living in a welfare state. Government intervention is thus required in the areas of social infrastructure development, as well as the provision of social services such as healthcare, education, employment, water purification, and industrialization. This is the main reason why government spending in the 20th century skyrocketed. The study of government spending has so become more popular. Public or government expenditure refers to the spending of public authority, which includes federal, state, and municipal governments, as stated by the World Bank. Citizens' safety and economic and social well-being are prioritized in these spending plans. In developing nations in particular, public funds are used for a wide range of projects that aim to improve people's lives and boost their economy. All fifteen people who took the survey felt this way.

Governments in developing nations are primarily responsible for quickening the rate of economic growth and development. As a result of the private sector's excessive focus on profit, quick economic development is impossible to imagine without government intervention. A strategy has been put in place to expedite the growth of the economy. In order to carry out the economic plan's set goals and objectives, the government invests a substantial amount of money. For economic growth, the government puts money into farming, manufacturing, and trade. Economic development is one of the reasons why public enterprises are set up. One of the social functions of government is to provide individuals with social services. For the impoverished, the disabled, the jobless, and so on, the government offers a variety of services. Health and unemployment insurance, old-age, widow's, and disabled-persons' allowances are all examples of this. In addition, public amenities such as parks, museums, libraries, sanitation, schools, and hospitals are provided by the government. The government spends money to provide these social services.

Classification of public expenditure refers to the systematic arrangement of different items on which the government incurs expenditure. Public expenditure can be classified as follows: -

1) Capital and Revenue Expenditure

2) Development and Non - Developmental Expenditure / Productive and Non - Productive Expenditure

3) Transfer And Non - Transfer Expenditure

4) Plan And Non - Plan Expenditure

5) Other Classification (Mrs. Hicks).

The World Bank depicts below the different types of public expenditure according to the economy-type and sector-type:

Table 3: Public expenditure

By Economic Type	By Function or Sector Type
Wages and Salary	General administration
Other goods and services	Defence
Interest	Education
Subsidy and transfer	Health
Investment in fixed asset and so on	Infrastructure and so on

Source: **Self as modified from Lewis (2013)**

A rising standard of living is characterized by an expansion in the quantity of products and services produced by a country's economy. Typically, it is expressed as a percentage of the growth rate of real gross domestic product (GDP). To remove the misleading impact of inflation on the purchasing power of consumers, growth is typically expressed in real terms, which are inflation-adjusted. "Economic growth" or "economic growth theory" in economics usually means the increase of potential output, or production while everyone is working.

Using models such as the Endogenous Growth Model, the Neoclassical Growth Model, and others, academics have identified a number of factors that contribute to economic expansion. Each of these models has its own unique set of assumptions that dictate how it will be put into action. Several factors have been identified as important for economic growth, and they are as follows:

1. Investment (Easterly and Rebelo, 1993)

2. Human Capital (Barro, 1991)

3. Innovation and Research & Development Activities (Aghion and Howitt, 1992)

4. Openness to trade (Barro, 2003)

5. Foreign Direct Investment (Hermes et al, 2003)

6. Institutional Framework (Rodrik, 2004)

7. Political Factors (Lensink & Morrissey, 2001).

8. Social Cultural Factors (Barro and McCleary, 2003)

9. Demographic Trends (Barro, 1997)

10. GDP per Capita (Barro, 2003)

11. National Income per capita (real per capita income)

12. Human development index and others.

However, it is important to approach the results of these research with caution, as not all public initiatives are designed to promote economic growth and public spending are not the only factor that matters for economic growth. Beyond that, it's not always the case that government spending leads to more economic growth. Although public spending has an effect on GDP growth, GDP expansion can cause shifts in public spending overall (as seen in Wagner's Law, for instance) or in specific areas (as seen in changes in demand for certain public services, for example). Public spending's effect on GDP growth has been the subject of numerous empirical investigations using time-series or cross-national data. While some research finds a correlation between government spending overall and GDP growth, other studies isolate the effects of certain types of government spending, such as public investment, education, or health spending, on GDP expansion. The main challenges that these studies face are the following: (1) determining the value of public sector outputs; (2) determining the impact of public expenditure financing methods (including the potential crowding out of private investment) independently; and (3) measuring the effects of other influences on economic growth. Furthermore, many public expenditure programs (such as those on physical infrastructure and elementary education) have extended gestation periods, thus it's possible that use contemporaneous cross-country statistics to link public expenditures to economic growth won't provide accurate results.

Wagner's Law of Increasing State Activity

Adolph Wagner (Booms & Greytak, 1969), the German economist made an in-depth study relating to rise in government expenditure in the late 19thcentury. Based on his study, he propounded a law called "The Law of Increasing State Activity".

Wagner's law states that "as the economy develops over time, the activities and functions of the government increase". According to Adolph Wagner, "Comprehensive comparisons of different countries and different times show that among progressive peoples (societies), with which alone we are concerned; an increase regularly takes place in the activity of both the central government and local governments constantly undertake new functions, while they perform both old and new functions more efficiently and more completely. In this way economic needs of the people to an increasing extent and in a more satisfactory fashion, are satisfied by the central and local Governments."

Wagner's Statement Indicates Following Points –

1. In progressive societies, the activities of the central and local government increase on a regular basis.

2. The increase in government activities is both extensive and intensive.

3. The governments undertake new functions in the interest of the society.

4. The old and the new functions are performed more efficiently and completely than before.

5. The purpose of the government activities is to meet the economic needs of the people.

6. The expansion and intensification of government function and activities lead to increase in public expenditure.

7. Though Wagner studied the economic growth of Germany, it applies to other countries too both developed and developing.

The respondents said that economic development of India can be improved through public expenditure by establishing good infrastructure across the country. The right allocation and stoppage of leakage will result in better results for public expenditure. The government should spend more on infrastructure. A large part of the money must go to lower class so that their socio-economic conditions improve.

Theme 5: Tax policy of the government of India (GoI)

Fourteen respondents rated the current tax policy of the government as positive, above average and excellent. Respondents also added that there may be a positive relationship between tax collection and economic development by proper utilization of taxes and acknowledgement of role of taxpayers. They added that rational taxation system helps in good revenue collection, and this consequently helps for economic development.

Some also added that developing countries have faulty taxation system, also full of corruption. On the other hand, developed countries run more sound system of taxation. In a poor country, like India more and more employment generation are required to spur growth and development. The object should be upliftment of those in last row. Development should be keeping those in mind.

Peter & Aderibigbe (2014) argue that the tax reforms of recent years in India are based on Chelliah's recommendations of simple broad-based taxes with a moderate and limited number of rates. The reduction in direct tax rates in the economy has not only increased revenue collection but also accelerated economic growth. This article aims to investigate the effect of India's tax policy on private capital formation. A time series analysis of data for the economy for the period 1950–51 to 1994–95 reveals that a one percent increase in the direct tax ratio has led to a reduction of 0.12 percent in the ratio of private capital formation to GDP. The article also examines whether there is any gain in opting for an expenditure tax to promote savings and capital formation in the economy. The major problem facing the Indian direct tax system is evasion of income taxes. The article concludes that an expenditure tax is a powerful tool to combat evasion.

Bernardi et al (2005) suggest that India is a federal republic and a big, highly populated and poor country, which however since some years has entered the catching up stage of development and shows impressive rates of GDP growth. General Government budget is structurally imbalanced and public debt stays high. Public spending (about 25 percent of GDP) is mainly devoted to general services, defense, and the support of economic activities, rather than to public health and welfare programs. Total fiscal pressure (about 17 percent of GDP) is in line with per capita GDP and is shared evenly enough between central and states governments. The structure of the tax system is not much beyond the Musgravian "early stage". A complex structure of taxes on goods and services is largely the main heading of the tax system and it is difficultly moving towards a VAT-kind structure. Direct taxes still are in an infant state, both as weight as well as structure. Import duties remain at not negligible levels. Social contributions are entirely lacking. A tax system of a country like India unavoidably raises more than one problem: foremost among these problems appear to be a too large dominance of a complex and obsolete indirect taxation and the fiscal relations among government layers. The road to updating and improving the Indian tax system has been entered since the early 1990s, but the reform is still largely to be accomplished. Introducing VAT – so successfully adopted in other developing countries – is the most striking but not the only example.

4.3.3 Content Analysis Results

Theme 1: Frequency of 'direct taxation' coverage in The Budget Speech

Table 4: Direct taxation coverage

Page Number	Total number of taxation word	Direct taxation	Percent
22-25-35	9	5	55.5%

This table indicates the number of times the word 'taxation' occurs in the report by the Ministry of Finance. The frequency of direct taxation is only 55%.

Theme 2: Frequency of 'indirect taxation' coverage in The Indian Economy

Table 5: Indirect taxation coverage

Page Number	Total number of taxation word	Indirect taxation	Percent
23-27-30-55	9	4	44.4%

This table indicates that the frequency of 'indirect taxation' is 44.4%. Indirect taxes have been given sufficient weightage in the report.

Theme 3: Section-wise coverage of 'tax' in The Budget Speech

Table 6: Section-wise coverage of the word 'tax'

Sections	Page Number	Percent
Section 1 (Introduction)	1	0/134 (0%)
Section 2 (Global Context)	1	0/134 (0%)
Section 3 (Interim Budget)	2	0/134 (0%)
Section 4 (Budget Theme)	2	0/134 (0%)
Section 5 (Budget Priorities)	2	2/134 (1.5%)
Section 6 (Budget Estimates)	20	7/134 (5.2%)
Section 7 (Part B)	22	125/134 (93.2%)

This table indicates the different sections in which the word 'tax' has been discussed. This directs one to the fact that taxation is an important point of discussion in annual budgets of the country. However, it is neglected in a few sections of the Budget.

Section 1 deals with the Introduction; Section 2 deals with global context; Section 3 discusses Interim Budget while Section 4 discusses the Budget Theme and Section 5 the Budget Priorities; finally Section 6 deals with Budget Estimates 2024-25; Section 7 is Part B dealing with annexures and miscellaneous forms of taxation.

Theme 4: Placement of 'development' in The Budget Speech

Table 7: Placement of the word 'development'

Sections	Page Number	Total Percent
Section 1 (Introduction)	1	2/57 (3.5%)
Section 2 (Global Context)	1	0/57 (0%)
Section 3 (Interim Budget)	3	0/57 (0%)
Section 4 (Budget Theme)	4	0/57 (0%)
Section 5 (Budget Priorities)	5	45/57 (78.9%)
Section 6 (Budget Estimates)	20	4/57 (7.01%)
Section 7 (Part B)	22	6/57 (10.5%)

This table signifies the importance of the word 'development'. It has been covered in different ways under different sections. Section 1 deals with Introduction; Section 2 deals with Global Context; Section 3 discusses Interim Budget; Section 4 discusses the Budget Theme; Section 5 spells out Budget Priorities;

Section 6 explains Budget Estimates and Section 7 is Part B of the Budget.

Theme 5: Main types of taxes discussed in different sections

Table 8: Main types of taxes

Type of tax	Page Number	Total Percent
GST/Indirect taxes	1-62	4/134 (3%)
Income/Direct taxes	1-62	9/134 (6.7%)
Corporate/Other taxes	1-62	3/134 (2.2%)

This table indicates that the different types of taxes discussed across different sections has different importance across the pages. While GST has 3% weightage, direct taxes have 6.7% weightage and corporate and other taxes are only 2.2% in importance. This indicates that taxes have not been discusses in such detail in the Budget Speech and has little mention in the FM's discussion around national finances and resources.

Theme 6: Developmental coding themes of discussion in different sections

Table 9: Welfare themes in different sections

Developmental theme	Section	Total Percent
Expenditure	All	9/72 (12.5%)
Welfare	All	1/72 (1.4%)
Revenue	All	5/72 (7.0%)
Development	All	57/72 (79.1%)

This table indicates the salience of issues across the report. Since the study discusses the effect of taxation on economic development of India, the different developmental themes discussed in different sections are expenditure, welfare, revenue and the word 'development' with development getting the focus at 79% of weightage. It is disappointing to note that the word 'welfare' occurs only once in the entire speech and such themes have been missing from the FM's discussion of national resources, receipts, expenditures and budget.

Theme 7: Themes showcasing growth impacted by taxation

Table 10: 'Growth' theme impacted by taxation

Section	Page Number	Total Percent
Section 1 (Introduction)	1	0/10 (0%)
Section 2 (Global Context)	1	2/10 (20%)
Section 3 (Interim Budget)	2	0/10 (0%)
Section 4 (Budget Theme)	2	0/10 (0%)
Section 5 (Budget Priorities)	2	7/10 (70%)
Section 6 (Budget Estimates)	20	0/10 (0%)
Section 7 (Part B)	22	1/10 (10%)

This table informs the reader about how often 'growth' word has been discussed. To repeat, Section 1 deals with the Introduction of the Budget Speech. Section 2 deals with the Global Context. Section 3 discusses Interim Budget while Section 4 discusses the Budget Theme. Section 5 spells out Budget Priorities and

Section 6 and Section 7 discuss Budget Estimates and Part B respectively.

Growth has been used the most under Budget Priorities at 70%; followed by Global Context at 20%. The word could have been discussed a greater number of times, however, it has not been discussed sufficient number of times in the Budget Speech.

4.4 Triangulation of the Results

Triangulation tends to enrich the study. Using semi-structured interviews, observations, and documents from the literature review provides different datasets to illustrate various aspects of the study phenomenon. It helps to validate the hypothesis when one set of numerous data set were included, which comprises semi-structured exploratory interviews with 15 tax officials and variety of perspectives of experiences and perceptions of tax implications and economic development. The multiple approach triangulation strategy promotes many methods for collecting data, according to Denzin (1970).

Phase one of triangulation concentrated on understanding the context of the study. It included interviews with several tax officials' and lawyers' mindsets on what is a good tax strategy, what is economic development and what is good public expenditure.

The second phase involves document reviews related to the study's literature drawing on implicit theories on public expenditure and the role of government spending on economic development and growth of a country.

Data from the interviews are evaluated using techniques consistent with qualitative exploratory study. The data were coded and analyzed thematically. The themes that emerged from the interview guide and document analysis were forwarded to the study participants for their feedback and validated through the literature review.

Finally, the findings were supplemented by the interviews and the literature review's similarities. A thorough document search was done, including, but not limited to, research documents, media reports and papers, reports by the government of India's Ministry of Finance, declarations of government policy, and publications published on taxation and role of government in development of a nation. This data is used to validate and affirm the effects taxation on economic development. Hence the hypothesis that effect of taxation leads to economic development of the country is proven.

To achieve credibility Proctor (2017) indicated that the study must ensure the accuracy, richness, and trustworthiness of the data rather than the data's quantity. The study cross-checked data interpretations with the research respondents from multiple perspectives. Using member checking helped to ensure the accuracy of the

interpretation of the data. Therefore, triangulation, which included coding and identifying tax officials' responses, shows credibility through constant engagement, constant observation, and external audits of the works through document reviews. These steps enabled cross-validation and encouraged analysis of issues impacting taxation and government spending on economic development.

4.5 Summary

This section provides a synopsis of the findings from the content analysis and the interview schedule. Development, growth, and taxation are all concepts that have been covered. The study's findings have been analyzed using triangulation.

Chapter 2 focuses on the literature review and conceptual framework, while Chapter 3 discusses the findings and how they relate to the study's conclusions.

Chapter V

Discussion

5.1 Discussion of Research Questions

The results show that taxing helps a country's economy grow. That's the first trend. Taxation is a major component of the Indian government's economic policy, according to the report's content analysis.

This chapter provides a summary of the results, analyzes how they relate to the current literature review, and draws connections between the findings and the conceptual framework.

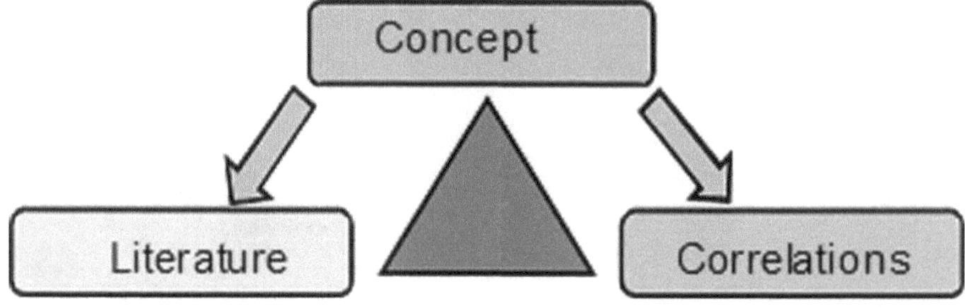

Figure 4: Review of literature, conceptual framework, and correlations

Themes, correlations, and literature reviews are connected in Figure 4.

5.1.1 Income tax and the growth of the economy

It is essential to find a good way to compare tax burdens because different tax systems have distinct characteristics, including national specifications, according to the OECD and WTI tax classification (Kotlan & Machova, 2012; Macek, 2014). This highlights the importance of taking the correct approach. Capital accumulation accelerates product growth until steady state is attained, as implied by the neo-classical growth model and various tax burden approximation approaches (Macek 2014). The purpose of this study is to provide evidence supporting this claim.

Capital accumulation accelerates product growth until it attains a steady state, according to this study's examination of taxation models. The opposite is true for government spending, which stunts economic expansion. This emphasizes how important it is to find suitable ways to compare tax loads

Regardless, contrary to expectations, the results showed that government spending stunts economic growth. Some of the other significant findings included:

The tax rates of OECD countries should be reduced.

In order to make up for the decline in income tax collections, more indirect taxes must be imposed. The opposite is true according to studies that look at developing nations, especially those in Latin America, where reliance on consumption taxes seems to boost economic growth (Canavire-Bacarreza et al., 2013). For emerging nations like India, fiscal policies are of paramount importance, according to Neog (2018).

One developed nation is India in particular. Governments generate funds through taxes to tackle multiple challenges at once, including unemployment, inflation, price stability, GDP, balance of payments, and income and wealth inequality. The tax system is a tool for dealing with these difficulties. According to the author's analysis, which is based on optimum tax policy theory, tax policy has a consistent impact on India's growth performance (ibid).

Correlation to the conceptual framework

The economy's growth is influenced by changes in tax policies, as per Gale and Samwick (2017). Gordon (2016) and Summers (2014) both contend that direct taxes are a critical element in addressing long-term issues associated with the velocity of economic growth. In addition to this concern, Auerbach et al. (2018) assert that the federal government's long-term budgetary status is rife with complications.

According to Hinrichs (1966), a significant number of empirical generalizations regarding the size and composition of government tax systems were developed during various periods of socioeconomic development. This led to the development of a comprehensive theory that can account for all of these discoveries. The notion put forth by Hinrichs was not made public until 1966. A static cross-sectional analysis of many countries at once and a dynamic analysis of individual nations over several time periods were both used.

Researchers employed multiple regression to investigate the factors that affect the government's share of GDP in sixty countries between 1957 and 1960.

Using a cross-sectional profile, this investigation examines the structural distinctions between the components of current government revenue in 26 distinct countries. Utilizing (2) as a framework, we examined the evolution of these components over time, with a particular emphasis on the examination of tax systems in contemporary Japan, Israel, and India, as well as in a variety of African and Asian nations and ancient civilizations. Per capita income (an indicator of development), the extent of the foreign trade sector (a measure of openness), and cultural style (a comparison of "Northwest European" and "Mediterranean" traits) are the three factors that influence the change in tax policy. The theory that underpins the evolution of tax structures during development is encapsulated by this heuristic model, which is based on both static and dynamic analysis.

Olaoye and Olaniyan (2022) investigate the influence of income tax on the expansion of the Nigerian economy. In particular, we are interested in understanding the impact of Nigeria's VAT, CGT, and corporate income taxes on GDP. This investigation used an ex-post facto research strategy. A statistics bulletin released by the Central Bank of Nigeria (CBN) was reviewed in order to collect data pertaining to the variables under inquiry. An error correction model was employed to analyze the data for the study, which was conducted over a twenty-five-year period, from 1994 to 2019.

The results indicated that the model variables exhibit co-integration, a long-awaited relationship. The value-added tax, capital gains tax, and corporate income tax significantly affect Nigeria's GDP over the long term.

The study revealed that GDP is substantially and positively influenced by all of the variables. According to the report, the government is responsible for ensuring that taxes are administered and paid in a manner that is both efficient and effective.

In addition, if we are to increase revenue mobilization, it is imperative that we prioritize the collection of all qualifying taxpayers through strengthen direct assessment. The Nigerian government should reduce the country's exorbitant business tax, rather than eliminating it. This is because lowering taxes for businesses would boost wages and consumption by making more people want to work.

Discussion Related to Existing Literature

The degree and scope of the linear link between economic growth and direct taxes in OECD nations from 1996 to 2016 is evaluated in the study by Đurović-Todorović et al. (2019), which focuses on this relationship in particular. . This study uses GDP growth rate as a proxy for the possible relationship between economic development and various types of taxes, such as personal income taxes, corporate income taxes, and property taxes.

Đurović-Todorović et al. (2019) examine the years 1996–2016 in OECD nations to see if there is a linear relationship between GDP growth and direct taxes. They consider how various tax structures, including those on individuals, corporations, and property, might influence GDP growth. Increasing corporate income taxes is positively correlated with GDP growth and tax revenue growth in OECD nations, according to the research.

The weak association between property tax and GDP at the OECD level is, however, due to the tiny amount of property tax in the nations.

We have also calculated how much of an effect the rise in tax collections had on GDP growth in the nations that were the focus of our analysis. Results from the group correlation matrix show that OECD countries' tax revenue, GDP growth, and individual and corporate income taxes are all significantly related. Given the relatively tiny share of property taxes in OECD countries' GDP, it is not surprising that there is only a weak association between the two.

This analysis covers every country in the globe. This examination focuses on how this framework functions in India.

5.1.2 The impact of government-imposed taxes on economic growth

This theme delves into the impact of taxes on economic development, specifically looking at how direct taxation has contributed to India's prosperity. According to Gupta (2012), a developing nation must adopt an economic policy that encourages economic growth if it wants to improve social welfare and progress. Two major factors that put a strain on a state's budget are the growing political consciousness and the need for more public spending, both of which are prompted by investment plans that are implemented through inefficient processes.

Relationship to Theoretical Framework

There is no shortage of resources in emerging nations, yet these nations often fail to put their resources to good use. The main hurdles to advancement include insufficient savings and investment, limitations on foreign exchange, agricultural sectors that are underdeveloped, and human resource development that is inadequate. Domestic and foreign transmission routes can both be used to mobilize resources. Resources from outside the country can take several forms, including investments, grants, and loans. These resources provide the benefit of importing foreign resources by introducing modern technology. On the flip side, problem debt management could arise from depending too much on these sources. Financial resources such as domestic savings and taxation are examples of domestic sources. Taxation is a tool that the community has at its disposal to promote saving and investment. So, this is formally referred to as mandatory saving. Taxing spending while allowing savings and investment income to remain tax-free promotes investment in the private sector. It is not surprising that a state's overall financial health suffers when the state employs short-term measures, such depending on federal funds or using overdrafts. The goal of the corrective approach often put out by modern fiscal strategists to deal with the expanding deficit is to reach a satisfactory degree of financial independence. On the other side, the method of taxing is extremely difficult to put into practice due to its inherent inconsistencies. This is why a thorough assessment of a state's financial structure is necessary for an effective plan of fiscal restructuring. For this review, it is important to look at how well the tax system has done over time in two main areas: (i) collecting as much money as possible for the state coffers while still encouraging people to save and invest, and (ii) letting people put their money toward investments rather than spending it on themselves. To a large extent, neither the tax ratio nor the tax effort metrics show how the tax system reacts to changes in state revenue over time. Taxable capacity is not considered by the compound growth rate or marginal tax rates. Assessing the efficacy of a tax system requires looking at the tax responsiveness over time in connection to the buoyancy of taxation.

There was no measure in place to tax individuals at a rate greater than the Personal Income Tax from 1970 to 1980. Even before the economic changes of the 1990s, everyone could see that the tax system needed some serious streamlining. We were able to achieve this increase in revenue productivity by drastically reducing the top marginal tax rates. There was a big structural change to the Personal Income Tax about fifteen years ago, when tax changes were first starting.

The top marginal rates of personal income tax have been lowered and the rate structure has been simplified. The impact of the change on the handling of individual income tax returns is now readily apparent.

There was a substantial increase in the exemption level, from 8,000 rupees in 1980–1981, to 1,540,000 rupees in 2007–2008, and a fall in the highest marginal tax rate, from 70% to 30%.

Discussion Concerning Current Literature

Rao (2000) suggests that the necessity of establishing a tax system that is consistent with the requirements of international competition is a substantial factor that has influenced recent tax revisions in a number of developing and transitional economies (ibid). The public's perception of the role of the state in development has undergone a sea change since the paradigm shifted from central planning to a market-oriented strategy.

To shift from an industrialization strategy that relies on import substitution and is centered around the public sector to one that is guided by market signals, we need to make significant changes to the tax structure. A tax system in an export-oriented, open economy needs to raise enough money to pay for social and physical infrastructure without causing too many distortions. Maintaining worldwide competitiveness would necessitate a tax system that can accommodate the demands of a market economy.

At least three distinct models of reform are delineated by conventional viewpoints on tax reforms. Ahmad and Stern's 1991 introduction of the optimal tax (OT) model is theoretically robust; however, its practical implementations have displayed deficiencies. Because of the complex relationship between tax policy justice and efficiency and the high administrative and information costs of developing an ideal tax model, the framework for directing tax policy is unworkable.

Similar to the OT model, the Harberger tax model (HT) is based on solid theoretical concepts. However, it is significantly influenced by real-world experience. This shows that when designing tax policies, administrative capacity is just as crucial as efficiency and distribution weights. This method emphasizes the importance of developing a system that is administratively feasible and politically viable, in addition to minimizing tax-induced distortions, rather than solely concentrating on the attainment of an optimal system. Harberger underscores the importance of tax reformers prioritizing best practice experiences in addition to economic methodology. A unified tariff and a comprehensive value-added tax (VAT) are two components of the essential HT reform package for developing economies that serve as market price takers. The third model is the supply-side tax model, or SST.

This model emphasizes the importance of reducing the state's influence.

As a theoretical framework, the Harberger tax model (HT) stresses the importance of administrative capacity in tax policy formation. The primary objective is to create a system that is both politically viable and administratively feasible, while simultaneously minimizing tax-related distortions. Harberger urges tax reformers to prioritize best practice experiences over an exclusive reliance on economic methodology. A comprehensive VAT system and a standardized tariff are among the components of the HT reform bundle that has been specifically designed for developing countries. In order to decrease public expenditure levels and the state's role, the supply-side tax model stresses the significance of lowering tax rates, especially direct tax rates. Proponents of this model argue for a larger tax pool with fewer deductions and preferences, all while keeping marginal tax rates low.

The objective is to minimize distortions in relative prices, with a particular emphasis on the preservation of minimal rate differentiation.

Cutting taxes, especially direct taxes, is crucial for reducing governmental spending and so reducing the disincentives to labor, save, and invest.

The importance of maintaining low marginal tax rates while expanding the tax base with limited exemptions and preferences is underscored by the proponents of this model. The primary objective is to prioritize minimal rate differentiation by minimizing distortions in relative prices.

5.1.3 Impact of indirect taxation on economic development

In the first theme, we examine how indirect taxes, such as the Goods and Services Tax (GST), affect GDP growth. While opinions vary on whether or not indirect taxes boost economies in developed countries, Ilaboya and Mgbame (2012) state that this is not the situation in developing countries like Nigeria. Their reasoning is based on differences in how they see the connection between the two. The investigation of the relationship between indirect taxes and economic growth in Nigeria is grounded in the endogenous paradigm, which supports a dynamic steady growth condition.

The endogenous growth model was popularized by King and Rebelo (1988). It posits that taxation and other forms of government action can sustainably boost per capita output through widespread innovation. The idea that government spending and taxes can affect output in both the short and long term is central to this model's political and economic significance. With the establishment of a strong correlation between taxation and GDP development, choosing the best tax system is no longer an easy feat.

According to the hypothesis put forth by Atkinson and Stiglitz (1976), the utility function can be split between labor and all items in a market where distinctions between people are solely defined by their ability to earn a salary. As far as the endogenous growth paradigm is concerned, this is correct. This being the case, direct taxes should take precedence in the ideal tax mix. The premise upon which the Atkinson-Stiglitz theorem rests is that people have a common set of qualitative characteristics. The output and resources of people may, however, differ substantially in practice. This leads one to believe that indirect taxation is the way to go when dealing with scenarios characterized by wide ranges in personal wealth. A general income tax is inadequate, argue Cremer et al. (2001), due to the reality that people's qualitative attributes could differ greatly. A number of commodities taxes, sometimes called indirect taxes, should form the basis of a successful tax strategy.

The impact of indirect taxes on investment is not enough to promote economic growth, as pointed out by Harberger, who conducted the initial research on this topic in 1964. This formed the basis of the investigation. Model analysis revealed that adjustments to tax components had no discernible impact on investment or labor supply, leading to negligible changes in economic growth. The main goal of the Harberger study was to investigate the impact of indirect taxes on the expansion of the labor supply. Using South African time series data spanning 1960–2002, Koch et al. (2005) conducted an examination. They looked at two main points: first, how taxes affect economic growth; and second, how the ratio of indirect taxes to total tax collection affects economic growth. An increase in indirect taxes relative to direct taxes has been found to have the effect of slowing economic growth. A study comparing the US and UK economies was carried out by Poterba et al. (1985). Between 1964:3 and 1983:4 in the UK and 1948:3 and 1984:4 in the US, they looked at the economic effects of moving from direct to indirect taxation. The study's conclusions indicate that, in the long run, imposing indirect taxes on the British economy reduces real output, drives up prices, and boosts after-tax wages in the short run. Having said that, the change does not significantly affect after-tax wages over the long run. Regarding the USA, a similar conclusion was found. In their 1996 analysis, Madsen and Damania replicated the work of Poterba et al., who had previously used data from 22 OECD economies spanning 1960–1990. Results showed that, for most OECD economies, shifting from revenue-neutral direct taxes to revenue-neutral indirect taxes had no long-term impact on economic activity. On the other hand, some people showed a different result. However, this study's findings are consistent with those of other studies showing that indirect taxes either have no effect on economic growth at all or a negative one.

Correlation to the conceptual framework

Musaga claims that there is a statistically significant negative correlation between indirect taxes and economic growth in Uganda (2007). Total and indirect taxes, say Greenidge and Drakes (2009), hurt Barbados' economic growth in the long run and in the short run alike. Using ARDL methods and quarterly data from 1990 to 2010, Scarlett (2011) evaluated a model that aimed to examine the impact of tax policy on the growth of Jamaica's economy. To promote growth in the long run, he decided that indirect tax increases would be preferable. The expansion of the economy may suffer if income taxes are raised to raise more money. In their examination of the Malaysian economy, Kadir et al. (2011) used quarterly data from 2000 to 2008 to determine the effects of indirect taxes and gross national products. While some taxes, like import and sales taxes, have a negative correlation with GNP, others, like service taxes, excise duties, and export duties, have a positive link. They reasoned that indirect taxes contributed to economic expansion. To examine the impact of indirect taxes on GDP growth, Ilaboya and Mgbame (2012) utilized ARDL methods for estimation in conjunction with data for Nigeria spanning 1980-2011.

Although the effect is not statistically significant, the results show that indirect taxes slow down economic growth. Using a VAR model for estimating and quarterly data from 2009 to 2017, Bâzgan (2018) examined the effect of direct and indirect taxes on Romanian economic growth. He discovered that although direct taxes have the opposite effect on economic growth, indirect taxes actually boost it. Using time series data from

1981 to 2018 and estimating with OLS and ECM approaches, Laura (2019) looked at how indirect taxes affected economic growth. He found that VAT and excise and customs duties work together to boost economic growth, which is statistically significant, but the effects of excise and customs duties alone are negligible. Indirect taxes have a little effect on GDP growth, but a large one overall. The long-term relationship between tax rates and economic growth was studied by Yanikkaya and Turan (2020). They used a panel data set for the Nigerian economy that covered the years 1970 to 1999 and applied GMM techniques to analyze the data. The researchers found that shifting tax revenue away from income taxes and toward property and consumer taxes had a favorable and statistically significant impact on economic growth, while keeping overall tax revenue stable.

Several countries, like Uganda, Barbados, Malaysia, Nigeria, Romania, and Nigeria, have shown that indirect taxes significantly hinder economic progress. According to research, increasing revenue through indirect taxes has a better long-term impact than increasing revenue through income taxes, which can have the opposite effect. Research done in Malaysia by Kadir et al. (2011) found that GNP and most taxes were negatively correlated, but GNP and service taxes, excise, and export tariffs were positively correlated.

A study carried out in Nigeria by Ilaboya and Mgbame (2012) found that indirect taxes had a detrimental effect on economic growth, albeit it is not statistically significant. Increasing indirect taxes promotes economic growth in Romania, according to

Bâzgan (2018), while increasing direct taxes has the opposite effect. According to Laura (2019), VAT and excise and customs duties work together to have a favorable and substantial impact on economic growth, but these two taxes alone have no discernible effect.

The long-term relationship between tax rates and economic growth was studied by Yanikkaya and Turan (2020). They used panel data for the Nigerian economy from 1970 to 1999 and applied GMM techniques. Transferring tax funds from income to property and consumption while keeping total tax revenue levels constant had a positive and statistically significant influence on economic growth.

Discussion Related to Existing Literature

According to Rahman (2023), several countries' economies benefit from goods and services taxes (TGS), including Bangladesh, Iran, Nepal, Turkey, Indonesia, Malaysia, Thailand, and Bhutan. On the other hand, Pakistan, Sri Lanka, the Philippines, and Japan see a detrimental effect on economic growth. Indirect taxes significantly and favorably affect economic growth in Asia, according to this study. In addition, because each country's economy is unique, the impact of indirect taxes differed greatly from one another. There is a strong correlation between political stability and GDP growth. In a politically stable environment, our study finds that indirect taxes bring in more money.

5.2 Discussion on role of GST on tax revenue collection

Both the first and fourth themes stress the significance of taxes and public spending in promoting economic growth and development in India. Findings point to a positive correlation between taxation and GDP growth in India. As a result, its accuracy has been shown.

5.2.1 The Goods and Services Tax and Its Role in Economic Development

When implemented on a national basis, the Goods and Services Tax (GST) constitutes a comprehensive tax system, as stated by Kawle and Aher (2017). This clearly signifies a significant advancement in the nation's development. With this massive change in taxation policy, we hope to unite state and national economies in pursuit of more equitable growth on a national scale. Currently, organizations and businesses face a plethora of tax levies that drive up product prices and cut into their profit margins.

The Goods and Services Tax (GST) has transformed taxation and helped the economy grow, so says Kawle and Aher (2017), making it a major achievement in national development. A more unified tax structure, lower spending, and better control of inflation are all goals of the Goods and Services Tax (GST). Ultimately, the goals of the GST system are to foster an atmosphere that is welcoming to businesses and to represent a substantial advancement in the reform of indirect taxes.

A complex taxation structure, together with a huge number of levies, is one of the biggest obstacles to the expansion of the national economy. Adopting the Goods and Services Tax (GST) system, which will lead to the formation of a unified tax framework, is a major step forward in overhauling comprehensive indirect taxes. One flat rate for all products and services will be put into place as a consequence of the GST framework. Many people think that by lowering costs and controlling inflation rates, the Goods and Services Tax (GST) will create an environment that is conducive to business.

According to Naeem and Khan (2020), the Goods and Services Tax in India was put into effect on July 1, 2017. When Shri Atal Bihari Vajpayee was India's prime minister in 2000, he ordered the Goods and Services Tax to be put into effect. It is official: the government has formed a committee to model the Goods and Services Tax (GST) comprehensively. The initial suggestion for a nationwide GST was made during the speech delivered following the presentation of the budget in April of 2006. Products and services, along with all other parts of the economy, were to be subject to the Goods and Services Tax (GST) when the 115th Constitution Amendment Bill was presented to the Lok Sabha in 2011. In 2014, the Lok Sabha ratified the 122nd Amendment to the Constitution. On August 3, 2016, the Rajya Sabha passed the Goods and Services Tax (GST). In September 2016, the approval to implement the Goods and Services Tax (GST) was given by the President of India. On September 22, 2016, the GST council came into being. Great success has been achieved in India with the implementation of the Goods and Services Tax (GST).

Among all countries surveyed, India has the highest Goods and Services Tax (GST) rates.

The Goods and Services Tax (GST) was a major overhaul to India's indirect tax system that eliminated duplication of taxes and other barriers to trade between states. The implementation of the GST is to blame for this. Lower levels of competition amongst the states may result from this. Deploying the uniform tax framework across countries has been completed successfully. By attracting more investment, boosting exports, and creating more job possibilities, it may help the Indian economy grow. Additionally, in an effort to better manage India's indirect tax system, the consumption-based Goods and Services Tax (GST) is now being put into place. The Goods and Services Tax (GST) might boost India's global competitiveness if it is effectively put into place. The Goods and Services Tax (GST) regulates the implementation and management of indirect taxes through its five-tiered structure:0%,5%,12%,18%, and 28%.

Many areas of India's economy have felt the effects of the Goods and Services Tax's (GST) new indirect tax rates. A number of socioeconomic facets of people's lives have been impacted by the Goods and Services Tax (GST), which has also had an impact on the country's social units, and more especially its residents. Several products have had their tax rates reduced as a result of the Goods and Services Tax (GST). Products such as these are categorized as follows: curd, organic honey, flour, packaged foods, shoes, tea, spices, pizza dough, cornflakes, ice cream, printers, hair products, and pre-owned automobiles.

A side effect of the Goods and Services Tax (GST) is a decrease in the taxes that are imposed on services like tailoring, private LPG distribution, and admission to entertainment venues and theme parks. In addition to necessities, the ordinary population relies on these products and services on a regular basis.

People also hope that the town's social life will improve if the taxes on theme parks are reduced. Some items now have higher tax rates than they had before. Anything from clothes to cell phones to raincoats to plywood to mattresses to detergents to telecommunications to water heaters to dishwashers to vacuum cleaners to cars is among these things. All things considered, these luxuries serve as symbols of one's social status. A notable spike in inflation over the last several months has also been caused by the Goods and Services Tax (GST). In light of the many unknowns surrounding the GST's adoption, several businesses have raised prices. The CPI inflation rate increased from 1.54% in June 2017 to 3.36% in August 2017. In addition, the pattern of rising inflation in the Indian economy, which started in July 2016, peaked in December 2017. Rules to prevent people from taking advantage of the system are laid forth in the Goods and Services Tax (GST) legislation. The law's stated goal is to mitigate inflation's effect on India's economy by ensuring that consumers reap the rewards of any gains made.

5.2.2 Startups, investments, and the effects of taxes on economic growth

The number of Indians with their own businesses has been on the rise in recent years, and the effect of these new ventures on the country's economy is growing rapidly. From 15,000 in the 1980s to around 100,000 in the 2010s, the number of new company registrations increased dramatically, driven by strong demographics and a business-friendly commercial environment. The average age of a business owner in India is 28, making it one of the world's youngest startup communities. The IBM Institute for Business Value and Oxford Economics collaborated on a poll that drew over 1,300 Indian CEOs. Around 600 startup founders, 100 VCs, 100 government officials, 500 business executives, and 22 school heads gathered to study India's burgeoning startup scene and its effects on the country's economy. Findings from the poll indicate that new businesses in India can take advantage of several characteristics and benefits that are unique to the nation. Of the Indian executives surveyed, 76 percent cited the country's open economy as a major plus for companies, while 60 percent cited the availability of skilled workers as a key strength. These two features are highly prized for their own merits. Half of the people who took part in the survey think there are a lot of benefits to tapping into India's massive home market. The fast expansion of new businesses in India has been good for the country's economy and its overall financial development. At an alarming rate, new businesses are expanding their reach outside conventional regions and into regional economies. The rise of creative new companies has two effects: first, it creates new markets; second, it disrupts established business paradigms. New companies in several industries represent a serious challenge to more established ones and to the conventional methods of distribution. Their inventive qualities allow them to play a catalyst role in India's corporate ecosystems, fostering collaboration and new ideas.

Analysis of Current Literature

There are now an estimated 38,756 newly recognized firms in India. This statistic includes a total of 27 unicorns, with 8 of them having achieved this status in 2020. Consistently ranked third globally, it is a mecca for tech startups. There is a great deal of hope for the growth of a robust ecosystem conducive to the launch of new businesses in India as a result of the country's economy, demographic trends, and the government's proactive backing. India can now take the lead in the world when it comes to launching new companies, thanks to this.

- The Economic Climate in India Before the COVID-19 pandemic. Consistent expansion and subsequent sustained increases in purchasing power were hallmarks of the Indian economy prior to the dramatic disruption caused by the COVID-19 pandemic. Before the unexpected shutdown, this was the state of the economy. Forecasts indicate that spending will increase due to the growth of the high- and upper-middle-income demographics, which will lead to an economic recovery in the near future. This is anticipated to take place very soon. Entrepreneurs in India have a lot of room to grow their businesses thanks to the massive potential of the Indian market. A major benefit that may be described as such is the demographics of the Indian people. Nearly half of the country's population is predicted to be under the age of 25. Approximately 700 million individuals were born between the years of 2000 and the late '80s, making them a generation with disposable income and aspirations for material possessions. These people can aim for tangible things. Also, this is a sizable demographic that has the purchasing power to try out new services and products offered by entrepreneurs. This constitutes a substantial demographic in this regard.

Help from the federal government: In 2016, the Indian government opened up the "Startup India" program to new companies in the early stages of their development. The program's overarching goal is to facilitate the establishment of a robust ecosystem that sparks a revolution in the realm of entrepreneurship and encourages the launch of new firms.

Innovation on the side of the state is the main factor causing the digital payment ecosystem to change. Aadhaar, Jan Dhan, UPI, and India Stack are utilized by the National Payments Corporation of India (NPCI). This assertion is significant.

Reduced barriers to entry into the industry have resulted from the expansion of digital connection in India. Because of this, a favorable setting has emerged, perfect for the launch of new enterprises. A great deal of opportunity exists in rural locations for: Numerous new companies are focusing on raising the quality of life in rural parts of India because a large portion of the population still lives there.

"The government of India initiated the Startup India program in January 2016," Singh (2021) reports. Upon its introduction, this program had a profound effect on how markets, prospective entrepreneurs, and investors saw businesses. This adjustment was the result of multiple legislative initiatives aimed at creating a climate that is friendly to the launch of new companies. Motivating younger people to become "job creators" instead of "job seekers" and to take chances with their ideas was the goal of these policies. To take advantage of India's demographic dividend, it was critical to put the country's people resources to good use. An initiative developed with the intention of increasing the likelihood of startups becoming successful, the Startup Action Plan (SAP) of 2016 primarily focused on three areas: providing financial support and incentives, streamlining the process, and fostering incubation and collaboration between academic institutions and the business world. Everyone knows that India has the third-biggest startup environment in the world, which means that this country has a lot of room to expand. A corporate culture that supports the launch of new companies has emerged as a consequence of several programs run by various governmental agencies, private companies, and educational institutions. We must thoroughly evaluate these programs to see if they tackle the core issues that need fixing in order to have a viable startup ecosystem, or if they only offer tax breaks and subsidies. In order to guarantee the success of the startup revolution, there are numerous factors that must be taken into account with respect to policy and regulation.

The Indian government's 2016 introduction of the Startup India initiative has significantly altered the startup environment.

The government's Startup Action Plan (SAP) project is tackling these important issues, one of which is creating an atmosphere that encourages new businesses to spring up and inspires young people to take risks and become "job creators." Issues of handholding, financial assistance, and partnerships between businesses and educational institutions are also being considered.

An example of India's growth potential is the country's recent rise to the position of third-largest startup ecosystem globally. But it's crucial to check these policies for nothing less than a comprehensive overhaul of the startup environment that goes beyond band-aid solutions like tax breaks and subsidies. This is necessary in order to ascertain the potential usefulness of these policies. Taken together, the policy and regulatory concerns are critical for a company's revival to be a success.

5.3 The Influence of Different Taxation Forms on Economic Development

In their 1991 article, Burgess and Stern suggest that economically distressed nations should consider implementing tax reform. Fairness and efficiency are crucial aspects to think about while assessing the overall condition of emerging nations' tax systems.

The inability of the government to amass sufficient funds to meet its investment needs is a major cause for concern in the Indian economy, say Rao and Sen (1995). The government's savings-investment gap has been widening for some time now. Government spending on infrastructure projects increased dramatically, going from 1.4% of GDP in the 1950s to 8.8% of GDP in the fiscal year of 1990-1991. This is the reason behind the dramatic growth. From the 1960s onward, the government's savings accounted for almost 25% of the total domestic savings in the economy.

This percentage, however, fell sharply, reaching a low of 4% in the fiscal year of 1990–1991. This chapter centered on the importance of different forms of taxation to India's economy, how they affect tax revenue and collection, and how that impacts the growth and development of the country's economy.

What follows is a brief summary of economic growth and development, followed by an analysis of its consequences for tax policies, a description of the study's limitations, and some suggestions for further research.

5.4 Summary

This chapter summarizes the previous discussions on the following topics: the relationship between income tax and economic development, the effects of direct and indirect taxes on economic development, the role of the Goods and Services Tax (GST) in generating tax revenue that supports economic growth and development, the GST and its role in fostering economic development, the impact of taxes on startups, the role of different types of taxes on economic development, and the positive correlation between the two.

Chapter VI

Summary, Implications, and Recommendations

6.1 Summary

The study's conclusion indicates that the research indicates a positive correlation between economic progress and taxes. This assertion is accurate, as indicated by the findings of the investigation. The theory that higher taxes have a positive and substantial impact on national economic growth and development is accurate, as evidenced by the data. This contributes to the expanding body of evidence that substantiates the concept. The study is informed by the theory of budgeting and the cost-benefit analysis models of a variety of models.

It takes into account transportation models developed by Tinbergen, McKean's studies, the Steiner Preemption model, and Chenery's SMP model and reinvestment, among others. This study also includes other models. This study also makes use of a number of other models. When seen through the lens of progress in the economy, the issues of structural unemployment and underemployment become research topics.

6.2 Implications

The study's implications are highly pertinent to the policymaking process, which includes assessing and analyzing government policies concerning taxation and economic growth.

6.2.1 Implications for Government Policy

We carefully read and examine all official government documents, including the report prepared by the Ministry of Finance. The study's findings are advantageous to economic development and growth, in addition to aiding in the formulation of tax policies by the government.

6.2.2 Applications to Practitioners

The study's results may be considered by decision-makers as they seek to establish new rules and regulations pertaining to taxes. For instance, OECD member states should lower their tax rates. More quickly and efficiently administered taxes is another important issue that the Indian government should address. It is also necessary to lower the tax on businesses. Governments should step up their efforts to eliminate income inequality and the disparity in the assets passed down from parents and grandparents if they want to see a decline in these problems.

6.3 Recommendation for Future Research

More research on the aforementioned topics is needed to guarantee that government policies work. These topics include ways to enhance tax administration, ways for tax authorities to incorporate reform measures, and what governments can do to make sure their policies work.

6.3.1 Limitations of the study

The study used a qualitative case study design and had a small sample size to investigate taxation policy. Finally, the study was completed. To take it a step further, we can investigate the tax policies that governments have implemented to boost citizens' standard of living by conducting a large-scale quantitative or mixed-method study. People in the country can enjoy a higher standard of living if this is done. In the future, researchers will be able to use a wider range of models to study economic growth and development if their projects use mixed approaches. The advent of hybrid research has made this a realistic goal.

6.4 Conclusion

So, to address the difficulties and issues that India's tax policy is facing, the study expands upon the prior efforts of academics and theorists who have sought to integrate the most effective tax strategies in both developing and developed nations. The study's principal goal is to identify causes and potential solutions to India's challenges. It is possible that the results and the conclusions will affect the expansion and improvement of the economy.

References

Abdullah, M. D. F., Ardiansah, M. N., & Hamidah, N. (2017). The effect of company size, company age, public ownership and audit quality on internet financial reporting. *Sriwijaya international journal of dynamic economics and business*, 153-166.

Adema, M. (2008, July). Budgeting under expenditure rules in the Netherlands. In *presentato al Workshop internazionale su "Disciplina di bilancio ed efficienza del settore pubblico", organizzato dal Servizio Studi del Dipartimento della Ragioneria generale dello Stato* (pp. 10-11).

Aghion, P., & Howitt, P. (1996). Research and development in the growth process. *Journal of Economic Growth*, 1, 49-73.

Ahmad, E., Ahmad, E., & Stern, N. (1991). *The theory and practice of tax reform in developing countries*. Cambridge University Press.

Ahmed, S., & Gillwald, A. (2020). Multifaceted Challenges of Digital Taxation in Africa.

Akhor, S. O. (2014). Impact of tax revenue on economic growth in Nigeria.(An unpublished M. Sc. thesis). *Department of Accounting, University of Benin, Benin-City, Edo State, Nigeria.*

Akhor, S. O., & Ekundayo, O. U. (2016). The impact of indirect tax revenue on economic growth: The Nigeria experience. *Igbinedion University Journal of Accounting*, 2(08), 62-87.

Anyanwu, J. C. (1999). Fiscal Relations among the various Tiers of Government in Nigeria. In *Fiscal Federalism and Nigerian's Economic Development, NES selected Papers Presented at the 1999 Annual conference, Ibadan.*

Armingeon, K., & Beyeler, M. (Eds.). (2004). *The OECD and European welfare states*. Edward Elgar Publishing.

Atkinson, A. B., Gordon, J. P., & Harrison, A. (1989). Trends in the shares of top wealth-holders in Britain, 1923–1981. *Oxford Bulletin of Economics and Statistics*, *51*(3), 315-332.

Atkinson, A. B., & Stiglitz, J. E. (1976). The design of tax structure: direct versus indirect taxation. *Journal of public Economics*, 6(1-2), 55-75.

Auerbach, A. J., Gale, W. G., & Krupkin, A. (2018). The federal budget outlook: even crazier after all these years. *Retrieved July*, 27, 2018.

Barro, R. J. (1997). *Macroeconomics*. MIT Press.

Barro, R. J. (1998). Human capital and growth in cross-country regressions. *Harvard University*, 1-56.

Barro, R. J. (2003). Determinants of economic growth in a panel of countries. *Annals of economics and finance*, 4, 231-274.

Barro, R. J., & McCleary, R. M. (2003). Religion and economic growth.

Bauer, T., & Riphahn, R. T. (1998). *Employment Effects of Payroll Taxes: An Empirical Test for Germany*. IZA.

Bauman, A. (2015). Qualitative online interviews: Strategies, design, and skills. *Qualitative research in organizations and management: An international journal, 10*(2), 201-202.

Bâzgan, R. M. (2018). The impact of direct and indirect taxes on economic growth: An empirical analysis related to Romania. In *Proceedings of the international conference on business excellence* (Vol. 12, No. 1, pp. 114-127).

Bernardi, L., Fumagalli, L., & Gandullia, L. (2005). Tax systems and tax reforms in south and East Asia: Overview of the tax systems and main policy tax issues.

Bhatia, S., & Ram, A. (2023). Outsider at home: Reading babasaheb ambedkar as a radical, decolonial psychologist. *Journal of Personality, 91*(1), 14-29.

Bilgin, Y. (2017). Qualitative method versus quantitative method in marketing research: An application example at Oba restaurant. *Qualitative versus quantitative research*, 1-28.

Blundell, R. (1995). Tax policy reform: Why we need microeconomics. *Fiscal Studies, 16*(3), 106-125.

Booms, B. H., & Greytak, D. (1969). Wagner's law and the growth of state and local government. *The Annals of Regional Science, 3*, 32-40.

Bowden, C., & Galindo-Gonzalez, S. (2015). Interviewing when you're not face-to-face: The use of email interviews in a phenomenological study. *International Journal of Doctoral Studies, 10,* 79.

Burgess, R., & Stern, N. (1991). *Social security in developing countries: What, why, who, and how?* (pp. 41-80). Oxford University Press.

Canavire-Bacarreza, G., Martinez-Vazquez, J., & Vulovic, V. (2013). *Taxation and economic growth in Latin America* (No. IDB-WP-431). IDB working paper series.

Carone, G. (2005). Long-term labour force projections for the 25 EU Member States: A set of data for assessing the economic impact of ageing. *European Commission Economic Paper,* (235).

Chenery, H. B. & American Economic Association, Royal Economic Society, (1965). *Comparative advantage and development policy* (pp. 125-155). Palgrave Macmillan UK.

Cnossen, S. (1992). Key questions in considering a value-added tax for Central and Eastern European countries. *Staff Papers, 39*(2), 211-255.

Cohen, J. H. (2000). Problems in the field: Participant observation and the assumption of neutrality. *Field Methods, 12*(4), 316-333.

Cremer, H., Pestieau, P., & Rochet, J. C. (2001). Direct versus indirect tax: The design of the tax structure revisited. International Economic Review, 42 (3), 781-799.

Cyrill, M. (2022). Retrieved on February 19, 2024 from https://www.india-briefing.com/news/india-fta-2022-status-update-23513.html/

Daveri, F., & Tabellini, G. (2000). Unemployment, growth and taxation in industrial countries. *Economic policy*, *15*(30), 48-104.

De Haan, J., Sturm, J. E., & Volkerink, B. (2003). How to Measure the Tax Burden on Labour at the Macro-level?. *Available at SSRN 417347.*

Đurović-Todorović, J., Milenković, I., & Kalaš, B. (2019). The Relationship Between Direct Taxes and Economic Growth in Oecd Countries. *Economic Themes*, *57*(3), 273-286.

Easterly, W., & Rebelo, S. (1993). Fiscal policy and economic growth. *Journal of monetary economics*, *32*(3), 417-458.

Esping-Andersen, G. (1990). *The three worlds of welfare capitalism*. Princeton University Press.

Esping-Andersen, G. (2010). The importance of children and families in welfare states. In *The Future of Motherhood in Western Societies: Late Fertility and its Consequences* (pp. 125-148). Dordrecht: Springer Netherlands.

Fusch Ph D, P. I., & Ness, L. R. (2015). Are we there yet? Data saturation in qualitative research.

Gale, W. G., & Samwick, A. A. (2017). Effects of income tax changes on economic growth. *The economics of tax policy*, 13-39.

Galenson, W., and H. Leibenstein, 1955, 'Investment Criteria. Productivity and Economic Development', Quarterly Journal of Economics.

Gandhi, V. P. (1990). 9 Tax Structure for Efficiency and Supply-Side Economics in Developing Countries. In *Supply-Side Tax Policy*. International Monetary Fund.

Ganghof, S. (2000). Adjusting national tax policy to economic internationalization: strategies and outcomes. In *Welfare and Work in the Open Economy Volume II: Diverse Responses to Common Challenges* (pp. 597-645). Oxford University Press.

Gordon, R. J. (2016). Perspectives on the rise and fall of American growth. *American Economic Review*, *106*(5), 72-76.

Granot, E., & Greene, H. (2015). A estructural guide for Intervieviewing in qualitative research: a guide for Marketing, Technology and customer commitment in the new economy.

Greenidge, K., & Drakes, L. (2009). A New Measure of Taxation: An Application to Barbados. *Journal of Public Sector Policy Analysis*, *3*.

Gupta, K. (2012). Comparative public policy: Using the comparative method to advance our understanding of the policy process. *Policy Studies Journal*, *40*, 11-26.

Gustafsson, L. G. (1996). Lessening the Burdens of Government: Formulating a Test for Uniformity and Rational Federal Income Tax Subsidies. *U. KAn. l. ReV.*, *45*, 787.

Hallerberg, M., & Wagschal, U. (1998). Sustainable Public Finance: The Politics of Budget Consolidation, Tax Reform and Expenditure Control.

Hamermesh, D. S. (2005). Four questions on the labor economics of higher education. *University of Texas at Austin.*

Hancock, D. & Algozzine, B. (2017). *Doing case study research: A practical guide for beginning researchers.* Teachers College Press.

Harberger, A. C. (1964). Taxation, resource allocation and welfare, in NBER' and the Brookings Institution, The Role of Direct and Indirect Taxes in the Federal Reserved System. Princeton: Princeton University Press 25 – 75.

Hermes, N., Lensink, R., & Murinde, V. (2003). 18. Capital flight: the key issues. *Handbook of International Banking,* 516.

Hinrichs, H. H. (1966). A general theory of tax structure change during economic development. *A general theory of tax structure change during economic development.*

Holm, P., & Koskela, E. (1996). Tax progression, structure of labour taxation and employment. *FinanzArchiv/Public Finance Analysis,* 28-46.

Hunter, R. F., Christian, H., Veitch, J., Astell-Burt, T., Hipp, J. A., & Schipperijn, J. (2015). The impact of interventions to promote physical activity in urban green space: a systematic review and recommendations for future research. *Social science & medicine,* 124, 246-256.

Ilaboya, O. J., & Mgbame, C. O. (2012). Indirect tax and economic growth. *Research Journal of Finance and Accounting, 3*(11), 70-82.

International Monetary Fund, Annual Report, (1989).

Iversen, T., & Wren, A. (1998). Equality, employment, and budgetary restraint: the trilemma of the service economy. *World politics, 50*(4), 507-546.

Johnson, G. A., & Vindrola-Padros, C. (2017). Rapid qualitative research methods during complex health emergencies: A systematic review of the literature. *Social Science & Medicine, 189*, 63-75.

Judd, K. L. (1987). The welfare cost of factor taxation in a perfect-foresight model. *Journal of Political Economy, 95*(4), 675-709.

Kadir, J. A., Idris, M., & Mohamed, Z. (2011). Relationship between indirect taxes to Gross National Product (GNP): Malaysian case. *Business Management Quarterly Review, 2*(1), 28-37.

Kaldor, N. (1965). The role of taxation in economic development. In *Problems in Economic Development: Proceedings of a Conference held by the International Economic Association* (pp. 170-195). London: Palgrave Macmillan UK.

Kawle, P. S. & Aher, Yogesh L. (2017). GST: An economic overview: Challenges and impact ahead. International

Research Journal of Engineering and Technology, 4(4), 2760-2763.

Kemmerling, A. (2002). *The employment effects of different regimes of welfare state taxation: An empirical analysis of core OECD countries* (No. 02/8). MPIfG Discussion Paper.

Kenworthy, L. (2013). Rising incomes and modest inequality: the high-employment route. In *The Squeezed Middle* (pp. 31-44). Policy Press.

King, R., & Rebelo, S. (1988). Business cycles with endogenous growth.

Koch, S. F., Schoeman, N. J., & Van Tonder, J. J. (2005). Economic growth and the structure of taxes in South Africa: 1960–2002. *South African Journal of Economics*, 73(2), 190-210.

Kotlán, I., & Machová, Z. (2012). World tax index: Methodology and data. *DANUBE: Law and Economics Review*, (2), 19-33.

Laura, U. A. (2019). Impact of indirect taxation on economic growth in Nigeria. *International Journal of Advanced Engineering Research and Science*, 6(5).

Lensink, R., & Morrissey, O. (2001). *Foreign direct investment: Flows, volatility and growth in developing countries* (No. 01/06). CREDIT Research Paper.

Lewis, W. A. (2013). *Theory of economic growth*. Routledge.

Macek, R. (2014). The impact of taxation on economic growth: Case study of OECD countries. *Review of economic perspectives*, 14(4), 309-328.

Macek, R., & Janků, J. (2015). The impact of fiscal policy on economic growth depending on institutional conditions. *Acta academica karviniensia*, 15(2), 95-107.

Madsen, J., & Damania, D. (1996). The macroeconomic effects of a switch from direct to indirect taxes: an empirical assessment. *Scottish Journal of Political Economy*, 43(5), 566-578.

Malterud, K., Røthing, M., & Frich, J. C. (2015). Family caregivers' views on coordination of care in Huntington's disease: a qualitative study. *Scandinavian journal of caring sciences*, 29(4), 803-809.

McKean, R. N. (1961). Evaluating Alternative Expenditure Programs. In *Public Finances: Needs, Sources, and Utilization* (pp. 337-364). Princeton University Press.

Merriam, S. B., & Tisdell, E. J. (2015). *Qualitative research: A guide to design and implementation*. John Wiley & Sons.

Ministry of Finance, Government of India,, 2009. "Economic Survey 2008-9," OUP Catalogue, Oxford University Press, number 9780198064091.

Ministry of Finance, Government of India, 2024. "The Budget Speech". budget_speech.pdf, GoI.

Morse, J. M. (2015). Critical analysis of strategies for determining rigor in qualitative inquiry. *Qualitative health research*, 25(9), 1212-1222.

Mujtaba, B. G. & Shoaib, S. (2016). Use it or lose it: Prudently using case study as a research and educational strategy. *American Journal of Education and Learning*, 1(2), 83-93.

Mukherjee, R. & Jha, P. (2023). Global Taxation and National Welfare States.

Murdock, S. H. (2019). *Applied demography: An introduction to basic concepts, methods, and data.* Routledge.

Musaga, B. (2007). *Effects of taxation on economic growth:(Uganda's Experience: 1987-2005)* (Doctoral dissertation, Makerere University).

Naeem, S., & Khan, J. (2020). the Social & Economical Impact of GST on Indian Economy. *The International Journal of Business Management and Technology*, 4(2), 74-85.

Neog, Y. (2018). Taxation and Economic Growth-A Critical Assessment of Literatures Specially Related to India. *International Journal of Research in Social Sciences*, 8(6).

Nickell, S. J. (2003). Employment and taxes. *Available at SSRN 489443.*

Okafor, R. G. (2012). Tax revenue generation and Nigerian economic development. *European journal of business and management*, 4(19), 49-56.

Okpe, I. I., Duru, A. N., & Stella, E. (2017). Effect of Tax Revenue on Economic Growth in Nigeria. *International Digital Organization for Scientific Research, 2 (3): 85, 103.*

Okwo, I. M., Uguru, L. C., & Nkwede, F. E. (2022) . PUBLIC SECTOR FINANCIAL PERFORMANCE AND ECONOMIC GROWTH IN NIGERIA.

Olaoye, F., & Olaniyan, N. (2022). A look into the influence of income tax, as a tool for stimulating economic growth in Nigeria. *Вестник КазНУ. Серия Экономическая, 139*(1), 110-120.

Oluba, M. N. (2008). Justifying resistance to tax payment in Nigeria. Economic Reflections, B(3), April.

Pande, G. C. (1996). Economic Liberalisation in India. *Indian Journal of Economics, 77, 27-40.*

Peter, Z. & Aderibigbe, T. J. (2014). The impact of tax accounting on economic development of Kano"s hidden economy. International Journal of Academic Research in Business and Social Science, 3(3) 113 – 125

Pfister, M. (2009, November). Taxation for investment and development: An overview of policy challenges in Africa. In *A Background paper to the Ministerial Meeting and Expert Roundtable of NEPAD-OECD Africa Investment Initiative* (Vol. 6, No. 2, pp. 11-12).

Phelps, E. S. (1994). Low-wage employment subsidies versus the welfare state. *The American Economic Review, 84*(2), 54-58.

Pissarides, C. A. (1998). The impact of employment tax cuts on unemployment and wages; the role of unemployment benefits and tax structure. *European Economic Review*, 42(1), 155-183.

Poterba, J. M., Rotemberg, J. J., & Summers, L. H. (1985). *A tax-based test for nominal rigidities* (No. w1627). National Bureau of Economic Research.

Pradhan, R. P., Arvin, M. B., Nair, M. S., Hall, J. H., & Bennett, S. E. (2021). Sustainable economic development in India: The dynamics between financial inclusion, ICT development, and economic growth. *Technological Forecasting and Social Change, 169*, 120758.

Proctor, S. L. (2017). Qualitative Research with Multicultural Populations in Educational Settings. In *Handbook of multicultural school psychology: An interdisciplinary perspective* (pp. 341-362). Routledge.

Proctor, S. (2017). *Strategies to improve job satisfaction and reduce voluntary employee turnover of nurses* (Doctoral dissertation, Walden University).

Rahman, M. M. (2023). Impact of taxes on the 2030 agenda for sustainable development: evidence from organization for economic co-operation and development (OECD) countries. *Regional Sustainability*, 4(3), 235-248.

Rao, M. G. (2000). Tax reform in India: achievements and challenges. *Asia Pacific Development Journal*, 7(2), 59-74.

Rao, M. G., & Sen, T. K. (1995). Public finance and economic development: Lessons from India. *Asia Pacific Development Journal*, 2(1), 25-44.

Rodrik, D. (2004). Institutions and economic performance-getting institutions right. *CESIfo DICE report*, 2(2), 10-15.

Saint-Paul, G. (1996). Labor Market Institutions and the Cohesion of the Middle class. *International Tax and Public Finance*, 3, 385-395.

Samuelson, P. A., Break, G. F., & Shultz, G. P. (1980). The Role of Government: Taxes, Transfers, and Spending. In *The American economy in transition* (pp. 617-674). University of Chicago Press.

Saunders, B., Sim, J., Kingstone, T., Baker, S., Waterfield, J., Bartlam, B., ... & Jinks, C. (2018). Saturation in qualitative research: exploring its conceptualization and operationalization. *Quality & quantity*, 52, 1893-1907.

Scarlett, H. G. (2011). Tax policy and economic growth in Jamaica. *Research Services Department, Research&Economic Programming Division, Bank of Jamaica*, 1-25.

Scharpf, F. W. (2000). Economic changes, vulnerabilities, and institutional capabilities. *Welfare and work in the open economy*, 1, 21-124.

Schneider, C. J. (2016). Examining elites using qualitative media analysis: Celebrity news coverage and TMZ. In *Researching Amongst Elites* (pp. 103-119). Routledge.

Sen, A. K. (1957). Some notes on the choice of capital-intensity in development planning. *The Quarterly Journal of Economics, 71*(4), 561-584.

Shaik, S., Sameera, A.S., and Firoz, C.S. (2015). Does goods and services tax (GST) leads to Indian economic development? Journal of Business and Management, 17 (12), 1-5.

Shirani, F. (2015). Book review: Anne galletta, mastering the semi-structured interview and beyond.

Silverman, D. (2016). Introducing qualitative research. *Qualitative research, 3*(3), 14-25.

Singh, V. K. (2021). Policy and regulatory changes for a successful startup revolution: Experiences from the startup action plan in India. In *Investment in Startups and Small Business Financing* (pp. 33-67).

Sivell, S., Prout, H., Hopewell-Kelly, N., Baillie, J., Byrne, A., Edwards, M., ... &

Nelson, A. (2019). Considerations and recommendations for conducting qualitative research interviews with palliative and end-of-life care patients in the home setting: a consensus paper. *BMJ supportive & palliative care, 9*(1), e14-e14.

Srivastava, S. K., Sharma, P., & Bhatnagar, V. K. (2010). Impact of changing scenario of taxation in India on tax revenue & GDP. *Journal of Accounting & Finance, 24*(2), 104-112.

Srivastava, S. C., & Teo, T. S. (2010). E-government, e-business, and national economic performance. *Communications of the association for information systems, 26*(1), 14.

Steiner, P. O. (1959). Choosing among alternative public investments in the water resource field. *The American Economic Review, 49*(5), 893-916.

Steinmo, S. (2002). Globalization and taxation: Challenges to the Swedish welfare state. *Comparative Political Studies, 35*(7), 839-862.

Stern, P. C. (1992). Psychological dimensions of global environmental change. *Annual review of psychology, 43*(1), 269-302.

Summers, L. H. (2014). Reflections on the 'new secular stagnation hypothesis'. *Secular stagnation: Facts, causes and cures, 1,* 27-40.

Swank, D. (1998). Funding the welfare state: Globalization and the taxation of business in advanced market economies. *Political Studies, 46*(4), 671-692.

Tait, A. (1999). Value-Added Tax, National: From The Encyclopedia of Taxation and Tax Policy.

Tinbergen, J. (1956). 'The Optimal Rate of Saving' in *Economic Journal.*

Tiwari, V. (2018). Effect of Taxes on Employment in India and World. *Journal of Management Research and Analysis (JMRA), 5*(01), 1.

Tong, A., & Dew, M. A. (2016). Qualitative research in transplantation: Ensuring relevance and rigor. *Transplantation, 100*(4), 710-712.

Vasanthagopal, R. (2011). GST in India: A big leap in the indirect taxation system. *International Journal of Trade, Economics and Finance, 2*(2), 144.

Venkadasalam, S. (2014, December). Implementation of goods and service tax (GST): an analysis on ASEAN states using least squares dummy variable model (LSDVM). In *International Conference on Economics, Education and Humanities (ICEEH'14)* (pp. 10-11).

Yanikkaya, H., & Turan, T. (2020). Tax structure and economic growth: Do differences in income level and government effectiveness matter?. *The Singapore Economic Review, 65*(01), 217-237.

Yin, R. K. (2018). *Case study research and applications* (Vol. 6). Thousand Oaks, CA: Sage.

Appendix A: Interview Questions

1. What do you understand by Goods and Services Tax (GST)?

2. How is GST a good form of tax revenue and collection?

3. How long have you worked with the taxation department (in years)?

4. What do you understand by economic growth and development of India?

5. How does direct taxation impact economic development of India?

6. How does GST and other forms of indirect taxation impact economic development?

7. How do startups and their taxation impact economic development of India?

8. Does corporate taxation and other inconspicuous forms of taxation impact revenue collection and economic development of India?

9. How can economic development be improved through better public expenditure by government? Any suggestions.

10. On a rate of 1 to 5 (1 being lowest/poor and 5 being most likely or excellent), how do you rate the current policy of tax collection by Government of India (GoI)?

11. On a rate of 1 to 5 (1 being the lowest/poor, 5 the highest/ most likely), how do you rate the tax revenue system and structure of different countries across the globe?

12. On a rate of 1 to 5 (1 being very poor, 5 being excellent), how do you rate a good public expenditure policy?

13. In which ways do you feel there maybe a positive relationship created between taxation and economic development?

14. What are your ideas, opinions, views on tax regimes across developed and developing countries. Please suggest any remedies to spur growth and development?

Appendix B: Interview Protocol

Interview: Tax policies to improve economic growth and development in India

The face-to-face interviews began with introductions and an overview of the topic.

A. I advised the participants I am sensitive to their time and thanked them for agreeing to participate in the study.

B. I reminded the participants of the recorded interview, and the conversation we are about to have will remain strictly confidential.

C. I turned on the recorder and distributed the Google form.

D. The interview lasted approximately 30 minutes to obtain responses for fourteen interview questions and a few follow-up questions.

E. I explained the concept and plan for member checking by contracting participants with transcribed data and requested verification of the accuracy of collected information as soon as possible.

F. After confirming answers recorded to the participants' satisfaction; the interview concluded with a sincere thank you for participating in the study.

INFORMED CONSENT FOR INTERVIEW

Taxation and Economic Development:

I, ... agree
to be interviewed for the research which will be conducted by
....
.... a doctorate students at the Swiss
School of Business and Management, Geneva, Switzerland.

I certify that I have been told of the confidentiality of
information collected for this research and the anonymity of
my participation; that I have been given satisfactory answers to
my inquiries concerning research procedures and other matters;
and that I have been advised that I am free to withdraw my
consent and to discontinue participation in the research or
activity at any time without prejudice.

I agree to participate in one or more **electronically recorded**
interviews for this research. I understand that such interviews
and related materials will be kept completely anonymous and
that the results of this study may be published in any form that
may serve its best.

I agree that any information obtained from this research may
be used in any way thought best for this study.

Date   *Signature of Interviewee*

Appendix D: Background Information of Research Participants

All tax officials and lawyers who worked with the Government of Uttar Pradesh, India